P9-DOB-974

THE ANCESTRY OF
Catherine Middleton

To Bartat Lee,

Clutzl C. Chv

THE ANCESTRY OF

Catherine Middleton

WHO WILL MARRY
PRINCE WILLIAM OF WALES
29 APRIL 2011

COMPILED BY
William Addams Reitwiesner

EDITED BY
Christopher Challender Child
AND
Scott Campbell Steward

FOREWORD BY
Gary Boyd Roberts

NEW ENGLAND HISTORIC
GENEALOGICAL SOCIETY
Boston, Massachusetts
2011

Copyright © 2011 by the Estate of William Addams Reitwiesner.

All rights reserved. No part of this publication may be reproduced or transmitted in any form or by any means, electronic or mechanical, including photocopying, recording, or any information storage or retrieval system, without permission in writing from the copyright holder, except for the inclusion of brief quotations in a review.

ISBN-13: 978-0-88082-252-7
Library of Congress Catalog Card Number: 2011923113

Jacket design by Stephen Bridges, *BridgesDesign@comcast.net*
Page layout by Anne Lenihan Rolland

NEW ENGLAND HISTORIC
GENEALOGICAL SOCIETY
Boston, Massachusetts
www.AmericanAncestors.org

To the memory of
William Addams Reitwiesner
(1954–2010)

CONTENTS

FOREWORD

Unlike Prince William – of Germanic royal, English noble, Scottish mercantile, Hungarian, American, and even Armenian ancestry – Kate Middleton has largely working-class ancestry from the English north. Her thirty-two great-great-great-grandparents include a solicitor, a master cloth finisher, a merchant, a pioneer of women's education (whose biography appears in the *Oxford Dictionary of National Biography*), a vicar, two messengers (one a prisoner in 1881), a clerk for the East and West India Dock Company, a draper, five laborers, a laundress, a butcher, a journeyman baker, two coal or ironstone miners, a shipwright, and a nurse.

Some of the northern families in Miss Middleton's ancestry are treated in C. A. Lupton's *The Lupton Family in Leeds* (1965). Her earliest known ancestor in the patrilineal line was her great-great-great-great-grandfather, a cabinet maker. A great-great-great-grandmother, Frances Elizabeth (Greenhow) Lupton, was a niece of the writer Harriet Martineau. Via the Martineaus—French Huguenot refugees to Norwich, at least three of whom were surgeons—Meadowses, and a Fairfax line of clergymen, Kate Middleton has knightly and baronial ancestry, including descent from Henry "Harry Hotspur" Percy, Lord Percy (of Shakespeare's *Henry IV, Part 1*), and Lionel of Antwerp, second son of King Edward III (who died in 1377).

Edward III's own ancestors include many of the kings of high medieval Europe. The mother of his *patrilineal* great-great-grandfather, King John of the Magna Carta, was the famed Eleanor of Aquitaine. Edward's *matrilineal* great-great-great-grandmother was Maria of Hohenstaufen, daughter of Philip, Duke of Swabia and King of the Romans (a son of Frederick Barbarossa), and Irene of the East, daughter of the Byzantine Emperor Isaac II Angelos, almost certainly by a Tornikes descendant of early kings of Armenia. Through these latter are possible descents from Cyrus II, Great King of Persia, the first Ptolemys and Cleopatras of Egypt (but not the wife of Mark Antony), and an uncle of the Athenian historian Thucydides. The Byzantine section of this line, the most likely link to the ancient world now known, appears in a long article by Don C. Stone and Charles R. Owens in the Spring 2011 issue of *Foundations*. Links to Persia, Egypt, and Athens were first developed in Mr. Stone's *Some Ancient and Medieval Descents of Edward I of England* (2003).

The Martineaus, treated in the 1972 *Burke's Landed Gentry*, are also in the ancestry of filmmaker Guy Ritchie, former husband of Madonna. (Kate and Guy are sixth cousins once removed.) A few Martineau descendants have immigrated to the United States, and a few others have become or married knights or peers. The social circumstances and hardships of Kate's nineteenth-century, largely working-class ancestors are depicted in Claudia Joseph's *Kate: Kate Middleton, Princess in Waiting* (2009). Another family of note in Kate's ancestry is Hobbes (via Davis and Lupton), treated in F. M. Lupton's *Descendants of Charles Hobbs* (1914); no connection to the philosopher Thomas Hobbes could be proved. A second once-thought gentry descent, through a William Davenport of Reading, doubted as early as the 1920s, is highly unlikely and discarded in the text of the present work.

Through Kate's fifteenth- or sixteenth-century Fairfax, Gascoigne, or Percy ancestors, Great Britain's next princess shares distant kinship with several colonial immigrants to the American colonies: Richard Saltonstall and Edward Carleton of Massachusetts; Mrs. Anne Mauleverer Abbott of New Jersey; William Bladen and Mrs. Anne Arnold Ross of Maryland; and Governor Edward Digges and Colonel George Reade of Virginia, plus Colonel Warham Horsmanden, also of Virginia, whose daughter married the first William Byrd. Descendants of these immigrants are not only all later Saltonstalls of Massachusetts and Byrds of Virginia, but also, via Colonel George Reade, a variety of notable Virginians, including George Washington, Declaration of Independence signer Thomas Nelson, Meriwether Lewis, and World War II commander George Smith Patton, Jr. Mrs. Ross was a great-grandmother of Francis Scott Key. Digges descendants include the wife of signer Charles Carroll of Carrollton; one of the latter's granddaughters married statesman Richard Wellesley, 1st Marquess Wellesley, brother of the great Duke of Wellington. Among Carleton descendants are the Pillsbury flour family of Minneapolis, and Saltonstall descendants include the novelist and aesthete Henry Adams, Bishop Phillips Brooks (author of *O Little Town of Bethlehem*), historian Francis

Parkman, illustrator Charles Dana Gibson (creator of the "Gibson Girl"), and novelist Louis Auchincloss.

Sir Thomas Fairfax, patrilineal ancestor of Sarah (Fairfax) Meadows, and his wife Agnes Gascoigne, both of whom died in the reign of Henry VIII, are also ancestors of the late Diana, Princess of Wales; and Agnes Gascoigne's parents, Sir William Gascoigne (d. 1487) and Lady Margaret Percy, are ancestors of the late Queen Elizabeth The Queen Mother. These two sets of ancestors provide Kate her closest kinships to both Prince William (fourteenth cousins once removed) and Queen Elizabeth II (fifteenth cousins).

This book's author and I co-wrote *American Ancestors and Cousins of The Princess of Wales* (1984), and I have updated that work with further noted distant kinsmen of the late Princess in *Notable Kin, Volume One* (1998), and several columns in the NEHGS *NEXUS*, *New England Ancestors*, and *American Ancestors* magazines. Richard K. Evans compiled an authoritative volume outlining *The Ancestry of Diana, Princess of Wales, for Twelve Generations* (2007, published by NEHGS). To Prince William's total ancestry, much expanded by his mother's forebears, marriage to Kate Middleton will provide a bit of new gentry, some French Huguenot and Scots, and a large amount of working-class ancestry to their future children: in effect, these children will have forebears from almost all classes in modern British society.

Most of Kate Middleton's forebears beyond the twelfth generation are (for now) untraceable, but the range of ancestry which may be carried by future British kings will now include most modern groups in the Anglo-American world, many early modern German princes, and various nobles in most of the states of late medieval Europe. Future royal marriages will also be of keen interest, and royalty studies in the later twenty-first century will require a knowledge of virtually all of western genealogy.

Gary Boyd Roberts
Boston, Massachusetts
March 2011

EDITOR'S INTRODUCTION

William Addams Reitwiesner began researching the ancestry of Kate Middleton soon after reports circulated that she was dating Prince William of Wales. With the help of Michael J. Wood of London, Bill gathered pertinent birth, marriage, and death registrations from the General Register Office (now part of the Office for National Statistics), and extracted British censuses from 1841 to 1901. Bill's research was labeled a first draft, and on his website he called that draft an exercise, treating a (not quite) random person born in the United Kingdom in the last two decades and tracing that person's ancestry largely via U.K. civil registrations and decennial censuses. With reference to a few printed works, Bill was able to trace nearly all of Miss Middleton's ancestry for two hundred years, following one line that led to the English gentry and then to earlier noble and royal families.

Bill died on 12 November 2010, and the engagement of Prince William and Catherine Middleton was announced just four days later. Over the years, Bill and I had worked on the ancestry of various twentieth-century figures, and several years ago he asked me to be his "literary executor," preserving his papers and publishing some of his research after his death. As Bill had co-written (with Gary Boyd Roberts) *American Ancestors and Cousins of The Princess of Wales* (1984), I thought a fitting tribute would be this work on the ancestry of Catherine Elizabeth Middleton, who will likely become Princess of Wales and then Queen of the United Kingdom of Great Britain and Northern Ireland.

Working from Kate's *ahnentafel*, available on Bill's website, *www.wargs. com*; reviewing Bill's papers in his home office; and with assistance from NEHGS genealogists, Scott Steward and I have edited this material and added further citations. Of particular note is the elimination of one sixteenth-century generation in the Fairfax pedigree — based on my research and that of Richard K. Evans — and the deletion of the gentry Davenport ancestry, following an e-mail report from John Wintrip. Bill was especially interested in matrilineal descents, and this work traces several generations of such ancestry (sometimes using pedigrees from the not always reliable Ancestral File). We have confirmed several lines with more substantial evidence, and a major goal of this study is to elicit further research. All additions and correction are welcome – e-mail *WmAddamsTrust@gmail.com* or send items to my attention at NEHGS, 99–101 Newbury Street, Boston, MA 02116.

This book is divided into two sections: an *ahnentafel* ("ancestor table") and kinship charts. To interpret an *ahnentafel,* see "About the Format" on page xvii. The charts outline Miss Middleton's kinships to a variety of notable American and British figures. Also included are various charts showing every monarch of England since Edward III and outlining several descents of the future royal family.

I hope you will enjoy this book as a tribute to the massive research undertaken by the late William Addams Reitwiesner. This publication, along with Richard K. Evans's *The Ancestry of Diana, Princess of Wales, for Twelve Generations* (2007), covers 75 percent of the known ancestry for several hundred years of future monarchs of the United Kingdom. I look forward to future correspondence and am pleased to honor Bill's memory with this contribution to royal genealogy.

Christopher Challender Child
Boston, Massachusetts
March 2011

ACKNOWLEDGMENTS

Several colleagues and friends greatly aided completion of this book before the royal wedding. I want especially to thank Gary Boyd Roberts for outlines of kinships to many notable Americans (and for his foreword), and Michael J. Wood, who helped Bill for several years on this endeavor.

Two other colleagues who aided Bill were Alan Merryweather and Robbie Wilson. Henry Bisharat, John Wintrip, and Richard K. Evans contributed valuable new research to this edition. Also useful were the online databases of Leo Van de Pas and George Larson, II. Jason Harrison and Emily Wilbur Alley checked microfilmed documents at the Family History Library. Julie Helen Otto and David Allen Lambert reviewed various internet sources and added material to the *ahnentafel*.

NEHGS Director of Publications Scott C. Steward added many citations and undertook further research on noted royal and English kinsmen. Penelope Stratton and Ginevra Morse of NEHGS consulted closely with us on the book's initial format, and Scott and I thank Anne Lenihan Rolland and Stephen Bridges for their work on the book's design and Sumanth Prabhaker for his assistance with charts.

Finally, for help in the monumental task of collecting and sorting Bill's papers in Washington, D.C., I want to offer many thanks to his sister, Dorothy Billopp Reitwiesner.

C. C. C.

ABOUT THE FORMAT

In an *ahnentafel,* each person is assigned a number, with the subject (in this case, Catherine Middleton) given the number 1. The subject's father is always number 2 and the mother number 3; paternal grandparents are 4 and 5, maternal grandparents 6 and 7, etc. In every father-mother pair, the father has an even number (n) and the mother an odd number ($n + 1$). The father's number is always double the child's number ($2n$), and the mother is always double the child's number plus one ($2n + 1$).

Thus the line from any ancestor in the *ahnentafel* can be determined mathematically, as the identity of father and child may be found by halving, or doubling, the number. For example, in this book the line to Sarah Meadows [No. 301], the subject of Anna Letitia Barbould's memorial poem "On the Death of Mrs. Martineau," can be worked out via her son, Thomas Martineau [No. 150], his daughter Elizabeth Martineau [No. 75], her daughter Frances Elizabeth Greenhow [No. 37], her son Francis Martineau Lupton [No. 18], his daughter Olive Christiana Lupton [No. 9], her son Peter Francis Middleton [No. 4], and his son Michael Francis Middleton [No. 2], the father of Catherine Elizabeth Middleton.

With this kind of numbering system, of course, numbers cannot be skipped, even when an ancestor is unknown. Thus the reader will sometimes encounter numbers followed by blank lines to denote unknown names.

LIST OF CHARTS

THE ANCESTRY OF
Catherine Middleton

List of Abbreviations

F.R.C.S.	Fellow of the Royal College of Surgeons
F.R.S.	Fellow of the Royal Society
J.P.	Justice of the Peace
K.C.B.	Knight Commander of the Most Honourable Order of the Bath
K.G.	Knight of the Most Noble Order of the Garter

Catherine Elizabeth Middleton

1. **CATHERINE ELIZABETH MIDDLETON,** born at Royal Berkshire Hospital, Reading, Berkshire 9 Jan., baptized at St. Andrew's Church, Bradfield, Berkshire 20 June 1982. On 16 Nov. 2010, her engagement to **FLIGHT LIEUTENANT HRH PRINCE WILLIAM ARTHUR PHILIP LOUIS OF WALES, K.G., F.R.S.,** elder son of HRH The Prince Charles Philip Arthur George, 21st Prince of Wales, K.G., etc., and the late Lady Diana Frances Spencer, was announced from Clarence House, London. They will be married at Westminster Abbey, London, on 29 April 2011.[1]

Well educated and stylish, Catherine Middleton attended St. Andrew's School in Pangbourne, near Reading, and Downe House School, Cold Ash (both in Berkshire), before completing her secondary education at Marlborough College in Wiltshire (2000). With Prince William of Wales, she graduated with upper second class honours from the University of St. Andrews in 2005.

HRH Prince William Arthur Philip Louis of Wales, K.G. (2008), F.R.S. (2010)

Born at Paddington (London) 21 June 1982

A focus of public attention since before his birth, Prince William of Wales prepared at Ludgrove School in Wokingham, Berkshire, for admission to Eton College in Windsor. After a gap year of travel and teaching, he went up to the University of St. Andrews in 2001, graduating with second class honours in 2005. Since then he has completed the graduates' course at the Royal Military Academy, Sandhurst, and an intensive course at the Royal Air Force station at Cranwell in Lincolnshire. He currently holds the rank of Lieutenant in the Royal Navy; Captain in the Blues and Royals regiment of the British Army's Household Cavalry; and Flight Lieutenant in the Royal Air Force.

First Generation

---

2. MICHAEL FRANCIS MIDDLETON, an airline officer with British Airways in 1980 and 1982, a company director of Party Pieces in 2011, born at Chapel Allerton Nursing Home, Leeds, Yorkshire 23 June 1949. He married at the Church of St. James the Less, Dorney, Buckinghamshire 21 June 1980,[2]

3. CAROLE ELIZABETH GOLDSMITH, an airline stewardess with British Airways in 1980, a company director of Party Pieces in 2011, born at Perivale Maternity Hospital, Perivale, Middlesex 31 Jan. 1955.[3]

The founders of a successful company supplying materials for children's parties, Carole and Michael Middleton live in Berkshire. Their other children are Philippa Charlotte Middleton (born at Reading 6 Sept. 1983) and James William Middleton (born at Reading 15 April 1987).[4]

Second Generation

4. PETER FRANCIS MIDDLETON, a civilian air pilot in 1946, pilot instructor (air service instructor) in 1949, an airline executive in 1974, born at Fieldhead House, Park Avenue, Roundhay, Leeds, Yorkshire 3 Sept. 1920 and died at Vernham Dean, Hampshire 2 Nov. 2010. He married at the Church of St. John the Baptist, Adel, Leeds 27 Dec. 1946,[5]

5. VALERIE GLASSBOROW, twin, born at 3 rue Giay Bompard, Marseille, France 5 Jan. 1924 and died at the Countess of Brecknock House Memorial Hospital, Andover, Hampshire 13 Sept. 2006.[6]

A graduate of Clifton College in Bristol who then studied at Oxford, Peter Middleton was seconded from his service as an airline pilot with British European Airways to fly with HRH The Duke of Edinburgh as first officer on the Duke's tour of South America in 1962.

6. RONALD JOHN JAMES GOLDSMITH, an engineer in 1953, a lorry driver (road haulage) in 1955, builder in 1980, retired maintenance builder in 2003, born at 57 Clarence Street, Southall, Middlesex 25 April 1931 and died at Brook Cottage, 14 High Street, Pangbourne, Berkshire 10 Sept. 2003. He married at Holy Trinity Church, Southall 8 Aug. 1953,[7]

7. DOROTHY HARRISON, a shop assistant in 1953, retired clerical assistant in 2006, born at 4 Mowbray Terrace, Sunderland, Durham 26 June 1935 and died at Royal Berkshire Hospital, Reading, Berkshire 21 July 2006.[8]

Third Generation

---

8. RICHARD NOËL MIDDLETON, an articled clerk in 1901, a solicitor in 1914 and 1946, woolen manufacturer and ex-Army in 1920, born at 9 Ottley Road, Far Headingley, Leeds, Yorkshire 25 Dec. 1878 and died at Fieldhead House, Park Avenue, Roundhay, Leeds 2 July 1951. He married at Mill Hill Chapel, Leeds 6 Jan. 1914,[9]

9. OLIVE CHRISTIANA LUPTON, born at Rockland, Newton Park, Potternewton, Yorkshire 1 April 1881 and died at 22 Clarendon Road, Leeds 27 Sept. 1936.[10]

> A graduate of Clifton College and Leeds University, Noël Middleton served as chairman of the Northern Philharmonia in Leeds. Olive Lupton was educated at Roedean School in Brighton.

10. FREDERICK GEORGE GLASSBOROW, a bank manager in 1920 and 1946, bank sub-manager (in Marseille, France) in 1924, born at 7 Grange Park Road, Leyton, Essex 17 Dec. 1889 and died at 12 Cordova Court, Earls Avenue, Folkestone, Kent 10 June 1954. He married at Holy Trinity Church, St. Marylebone, London 24 June 1920,[11]

11. CONSTANCE ROBISON, born at 8 Addison Road, Walthamstow, Essex 27 June 1888 and died at Olde House, Church Road, Penn, Beaconsfield, Buckinghamshire 19 July 1977.[12]

> Frederick and Constance Glassborow spent much of their married life in Valencia, Spain, and Marseille, France (birthplace of their twin daughters Mary and Valerie), before settling in

Leeds, where Frederick was manager of the Westminster Bank. He was later named a Freeman of the City of London.

12. STEPHEN CHARLES GOLDSMITH, a general labourer in 1901 and 1938, carman in 1909, house builder's labourer in 1931, born at Priory Road, Acton Green, Middlesex 6 Nov. 1886 and died at 57 Clarence Street, Southall, Middlesex 5 Jan. 1938. He married at Uxbridge Register Office, Uxbridge, Middlesex 27 March 1909,[13]

13. EDITH ELIZA CHANDLER, born at New Denham, Buckinghamshire 21 Jan. 1889 and died at Hillingdon Hospital, Hillingdon, Middlesex 1 Jan. 1971.[14]

14. THOMAS HARRISON, a carpenter in 1934 and 1953, house joiner in 1935, retired carpenter in 1976, born at 22 Nicholas Street, Downs, Hetton-le-Hole, Durham 23 June 1904 and died at 10A North Road, Southall, Middlesex 24 Aug. 1976. He married at St. Brandon's Church, Tudhoe, Spennymoor, Durham 12 May 1934,[15]

15. ELIZABETH MARY TEMPLE, born at 40 Salvin Street, Mount Pleasant, Tudhoe 20 May 1903 and died at Manor Court Nursing Home, Britten Drive, Southall 1 Dec. 1991.[16]

Fourth Generation

16. JOHN WILLIAM MIDDLETON, an attorney at law in 1861, a solicitor in 1863, 1879, and 1881, attorney and solicitor in 1871, born at Saint George's Terrace, Leeds, Yorkshire 11 Feb. 1839 and died at Fairfield, Far Headingley, Leeds 16 July 1887. He married at the Church of St. Peter-at-Leeds 27 Aug. 1863,[17]

17. MARY ASQUITH, born at George and Dragon Yard, Briggate, Leeds 15 Dec. 1839 and died at Hope Cottage, Filey, Yorkshire 22 Sept. 1889.[18]

18. FRANCIS MARTINEAU LUPTON, J.P., Alderman of Leeds 1895–1916, a merchant in 1880, cloth merchant in 1881, woolen manufacturer in 1914, author of *Descendants of Charles Hobbs, 1596–1700,* born at Potternewton, Yorkshire 21 July 1848 and died at Low Gables, Chapel Allerton, Leeds, Yorkshire 5 Feb. 1921; buried at St. John's Church, Roundhay, Yorkshire 9 Feb. 1921. He married at St. John's Church 6 April 1880,[19]

19. HARRIET ALBINA DAVIS, born at Roundhay 16 July 1850 and died at Rockland, Newton Park, Potternewton 19 Jan. 1892; buried at St. John's Church 22 Jan. 1892.[20]

A graduate of Leeds Grammar School and Trinity College, Cambridge (1870), Francis Lupton was the eldest of four remarkable brothers, each of whom contributed greatly to the civic life of Leeds. The others were Arthur Greenhow Lupton (1850–1930), Pro-Chancellor of the University of Leeds 1904–20; Charles Lupton (1855–1935), Lord Mayor of Leeds in 1915; and Hugh Lupton (1861–1947), Lord Mayor in 1926. Arthur and Charles married sisters; their brother-in-law

was James Bryce, 1st Viscount Bryce, the British Ambassador
to Washington 1907–13.

20. **Frederick John Glassborow,** a mercantile clerk in 1880,
commercial clerk in 1881 and 1891, writing clerk in 1886, ship own-
er's clerk in 1889 and 1901, shipping manager in 1920, born at 3 Nelson Terrace, Haggerston, Middlesex 22 Feb. 1859, baptized at St. Peter's
Church, Hackney, Middlesex 4 July 1880 and died at Homeleigh, Lis-
more Road, Beltinge, Kent 21 Dec. 1932. He married at the Church
of St. Mary the Virgin, Leyton, Essex 1 June 1886,[21]
21. **Emily Jane Elliott,** born at 4 Edward Street, Mile End Old
Town, Stepney, Middlesex 2 May 1859 and died at Homeleigh 13 June
1949.[22]

22. **Gavin Fullarton Robison,** a banker's clerk in 1871, 1881,
1891, and 1901, clerk in 1875, mercantile clerk in 1888, retired (bank) in
1920, born at 25 Nelson Street, Mile End Old Town, Stepney, Middlesex 2 Dec. 1844, baptized at the Church of St. James the Great, Hackney,
Middlesex 10 April 1859 and died at 21 Old Dover Road, Canterbury,
Kent 4 March 1925. He married at St. Matthew's Church, Sutton St.
Matthew, Lincolnshire 2 Dec. 1875,[23]
23. **Sarah Ann Gee,** born at Long Sutton, Lincolnshire 4 Aug. 1852
and died at Armside, Dundonald Drive, Southend-on-Sea, Essex 2 Sept.
1922.[24]

24. **John Goldsmith,** a labourer in 1871, 1882, and 1909, general
labourer in 1881 and 1886, navvy in 1891, bricklayer's labourer in 1909,
born at 3 Popham Street, Islington, Middlesex 6 July 1851. He married
at St. Mary's Church, Paddington, Middlesex 18 Sept. 1882,[25]
25. **Jane Dorsett,** living in 1911, born at 8 Paradise Row, Hammersmith, Middlesex 9 May 1861.[26]

26. THEOPHILUS BENJAMIN CHANDLER, a plasterer in 1868, 1871, 1881, 1889, 1891, 1901, and 1909, retired master plasterer in 1935, born at Malvern, Worcestershire 26 May 1848 and died at 8 Spencer Street, Southall, Middlesex 4 March 1935. He married at St. Giles' Church, Stoke Poges, Buckinghamshire 22 Nov. 1868,[27]

27. AMELIA WHITE, born at Iver, Buckinghamshire 13 Feb. 1846 and died at 8 Spencer Street 22 Nov. 1927.[28]

28. JOHN HARRISON, a coal miner in 1891, 1897, 1901, and 1904, a miner in 1934, born at Barrington Terrace, Hetton-le-Hole, Durham 25 July 1874 and died in County Durham in Sept. 1956. He married at Houghton-le-Spring Register Office, Houghton-le-Spring, Durham 23 Feb. 1897,[29]

29. JANE HILL, a domestic servant in 1897, living in Sept. 1956, born at Lyons, Hetton-le-Hole 28 May 1875.[30]

30. THOMAS TEMPLE, an ironstone miner in 1891, steelworker in 1894, farm hand in 1901 and 1903, called a gardener in his daughter's 1934 marriage record, born Tom Temple at Guisborough, Yorkshire 23 May 1871. He married at St. Brandon's Church, Tudhoe, Spennymoor, Durham 8 Sept. 1894,[31]

31. ELIZABETH MYERS, living in 1911, born at Hulam Sheraton, Easington, Durham 29 Jan. 1868.[32]

Fifth Generation

32. WILLIAM MIDDLETON, a solicitor in 1838, 1839, 1863, 1871, and 1881, solicitor and attorney 1841 and 1851, an attorney at law in 1861, born at Wakefield, Yorkshire 22 Sept., baptized at All Saints' Church, Wakefield 9 Dec. 1807 and died at Hawkhills, Chapel Allerton, Yorkshire 21 Dec. 1884. He married, 2nd, his sister-in-law Sarah Ward, who was baptized at the Church of St. Peter-at-Leeds, Yorkshire 3 Oct. 1819 and died at Hawkhills 3 April 1885, daughter of John Ward [No. 66]. He married, 1st, at the Church of St. Peter-at-Leeds 7 Feb. 1838,[33]

33. MARY WARD, born 29 May, baptized at the Church of St. Peter-at-Leeds 7 Aug. 1811 and died at Gledhow Grange, Chapel Allerton 15 June 1859; buried at St. Matthew's Church, Chapel Allerton 18 June 1859.[34]

34. JOSEPH ASQUITH, a cloth drawer in 1838, 1839, and 1841, cloth dresser in 1851, cloth finisher in 1861, 1863, and 1874, master cloth finisher and dyer in 1871, born 20 May, baptized at Queen Street Chapel, Leeds, Yorkshire 26 June 1815 and died at 215 St. John's Terrace, Leeds 9 Sept. 1874. He married at Queen Street Chapel 25 Oct. 1838,[35]

35. ELLEN WARD, sister of No. 33, baptized at the Church of St. Peter-at-Leeds 31 March 1816 and died at 6 St. John's Terrace, Leeds 16 Sept. 1888.[36]

36. FRANCIS LUPTON, a merchant in 1847, 1848, and 1880, cloth merchant in 1851, 1861, 1871, 1881, and 1884, born at Leeds, Yorkshire 7 Sept., baptized at Call Lane Arian Congregation, Leeds 25 Nov. 1813 and died at Beechwood, Roundhay, Barwick in Elmet, Yorkshire

20 May 1884; buried at St. John's Church, Roundhay 23 May 1884. He married at Hanover Square Chapel, Newcastle upon Tyne, Northumberland 1 July 1847,[37]

37. FRANCES ELIZABETH GREENHOW, a pioneer of women's education, born at Newcastle 20 July, baptized at Hanover Square Chapel 7 Sept. 1821 and died at Beechwood 9 March 1892; buried at St. John's Church, Roundhay 12 March 1892.[38]

Francis Lupton left Leeds Grammar School to work with his older brothers in the family firm. A magistrate for the West Riding of Yorkshire, he served as chairman of the finance committee at the Yorkshire College of Science, which would later become the University of Leeds.

Fanny Greenhow was educated in Liverpool (at the school of her maternal aunt Rachel Martineau) and in Nottingham. A driving force behind the establishment of Leeds Girls' High School, she served as Honorary Secretary of the Ladies' Honorary Council of the Yorkshire Board of Education, later the Yorkshire Ladies' Council of Education, from 1871 until 1885. Of her role on the council, it was recalled, "Enthusiastic herself, but not too enthusiastic—able to infuse her enthusiasm into others—she was the guide, philosopher and friend of all with whom she came in contact."[39]

38. REV. THOMAS DAVIS, Vicar of Roundhay, Barwick in Elmet, Yorkshire (1839), born 15, baptized at All Saints' Church, Worcester, Worcestershire 22 Feb. 1804 and died at the Friends' Retreat, Heslington Road, York, Yorkshire 11 Nov. 1887; buried at St. John's Church, Roundhay 16 Nov. 1887. He married at Holy Trinity Church, Stratford-upon-Avon, Warwickshire 10 Dec. 1839,[40]

39. CHRISTIANA MARIA HOBBES, born 25 Dec. 1810, baptized at Holy Trinity Church 15 Jan. 1813 and died at St. George's School, Roundhay 30 April 1899; buried at St. John's Church, Roundhay 3 May 1899.[41]

40. EDWARD THOMAS GLASSBOROUGH, a messenger in 1841, 1847, 1851, 1859, 1861, and 1871, prisoner in Holloway Prison, Islington, in 1881 (described as an "Insurance Co's Messenger"), "living on own means" in 1891, of independent means in 1898, born at Shoreditch, Middlesex 19 June, baptized at St. Mary's Church, Newington, Surrey 20 Aug. 1826 and died at 17 Vicarage Road, Leyton, Essex 11 Aug. 1898. He married at St. Mark's Church, Kennington, Surrey 13 Nov. 1847,[42]

41. CHARLOTTE ELIZABETH ABLETT, baptized at St. Mary's Church, Lambeth, Surrey 20 Nov. 1825 and died at 70 Vicarage Road, Leyton 21 July 1900.[43]

42. JOHN ELLIOTT, a messenger in 1841, 1859, 1871, and 1881, silversmith in 1843, clerk in 1871, called a gentleman in his daughter's marriage record in 1886, born at Cheshunt, Hertfordshire 22 June, baptized at St. Mary's Church, Cheshunt 19 July 1818 and died before 1 June 1886. He married at St. Mary's Church, Lambeth, Surrey 21 May 1843,[44]

43. ELIZABETH POWELL, born at Kennington, Surrey 30 Dec. 1815, baptized at St. Mary's Church, Newington, Surrey 6 Oct. 1816 and died at 21 Approach Road, Bethnal Green, Stepney, Middlesex 27 Aug. 1871.[45]

44. JOHN COCKBURN ROBISON, clerk in the East and West India Dock Company in 1844, called a clerk in his son's marriage record in 1875, called a mercantile clerk in his widow's death record in 1895, born ca. 1806 and died before 30 March 1851. He married at Irvine, Ayrshire 26 Nov. 1831,[46]

45. MARY NEWBIGGING, born at Irvine ca. 1803 and died at 20 Cedars Avenue, Walthamstow, Essex 30 Aug. 1895 aged 92.[47]

46. EDWARD WILLIAM GEE, a draper in 1846, 1881, and 1883, grocer and draper in 1851, 1852, 1861, and 1871, grocer in 1875, born at Bishopsgate, London ca. 1818 and died at Upgate, Louth, Lincolnshire

17 Sept. 1883. He married at St. Matthew's Church, Bethnal Green, Stepney, Middlesex 16 Dec. 1846,[48]

47. Elizabeth Marshall, baptized at Holy Trinity Church, Coventry, Warwickshire 7 May 1816.[49]

48. John Goldsmith, a labourer in 1850, 1851, 1881, 1882, and 1888, brick maker in 1861, born at Maidstone, Kent ca. 1827 and died at 2 Triangle Place, Islington, Middlesex 9 June 1888 aged 61. He married at the Church of St. John the Baptist, Hoxton, Middlesex 23 Sept. 1850,[50]

49. Esther Jones, a laundress in 1851, born at Ware, Hertfordshire 22 Jan. 1832 and died at 2 Triangle Place 19 Dec. 1885.[51]

50. James Dorsett, a labourer in 1845, 1861, 1871, 1881, and 1882, bricklayer's labourer in 1851, a laborer [*sic*] and road sweeper in 1891, born 6, baptized at St. Nicholas' Church, Chiswick, Middlesex 29 Nov. 1819 and died at 14 Paradise Place, Hammersmith, Middlesex 13 Feb. 1893 aged 71 [*sic*]. He married at St. Mary's Church, Acton, Middlesex 22 June 1845,[52]

51. Charlotte Mercy Powell, baptized at St. Nicholas' Church 13 Aug. 1826 and died at 14 Paradise Row, Hammersmith 21 May 1899 aged 72.[53]

52. Miles Tugwell Chandler, a butcher in 1841, 1844, and 1868, labourer in 1851 and 1881, mason's labourer in 1861, general labourer in 1871, born at Randwick, Gloucestershire 31 Dec. 1809 and died at the Beauchamp Almshouse, Newland, Worcestershire 14 Dec. 1881. He married at St. Swithun's Church, Hempsted, Gloucestershire 19 Feb. 1844,[54]

53. Eliza Jenkins, baptized at Upton upon Severn, Worcestershire 26 May 1817 and died at the Beauchamp Almshouse 18 Oct. 1896.[55]

54. URIAH WHITE, a baker in 1841, 1846, and 1868, journeyman baker in 1851, born at Bath, Somerset ca. 1806 (perhaps the Uriah White, son of Harry and Sarah, baptized at Brewham, Somerset 14 Sept. 1806) and died at Park Street, Slough, Buckinghamshire 1 Dec. 1867. He married,[56]

55. JANE BOWLER, a charwoman in 1871, baptized at Iver, Buckinghamshire 21 Dec. 1806 and died there 26 Feb. 1886.[57]

56. JOHN HARRISON, a miner in 1860, coal miner in 1861, 1871, 1874, 1881, and 1889, born at Byker, Northumberland ca. 1834 and died at 24 Lyon Street, Downs, Hetton-le-Hole, Durham 29 Jan. 1889 aged 54. He married at St. Cuthbert's Church, Shadforth, Durham 7 April 1860,[58]

57. JANE LIDDELL, born at Sherburn, Durham ca. 1839 and died at Lyons Street, Hetton-le-Hole 23 Dec. 1881 aged 42.[59]

58. THOMAS HILL, a shipwright in 1869 and 1871, waggon wright [*sic*] in 1875, joiner in 1881 and 1891, joiner (colliery) in 1897, joiner (changer and grather) in 1901, born at 19 George Street, Sunderland, Durham 17 April 1844. He married at St. Andrew's Church, Deptford, Durham 11 Oct. 1869,[60]

59. ELIZABETH WEBSTER, a dressmaker in 1869, born at Throston Street, Hartlepool, Durham 6 Sept. 1848.[61]

60. JOSEPH TEMPLE, an ironstone miner in 1861, 1871, and 1891, a miner in 1870 and 1894, iron maker in 1881, shopkeeper in 1901, born at Mickleby, Yorkshire 25 Dec. 1833, baptized at Lythe, Yorkshire 1 Jan. 1834. He married at St. Nicholas' Church, Guisborough, Yorkshire 11 April 1870,[62]

61. HARRIET STONE, born at Jones' Yard, High Street, King's Lynn, Norfolk 17 Nov. 1851.[63]

62. JOSEPH MYERS, a labourer in 1850, an agricultural labourer in 1851, 1881, and 1891, hind or farm labourer in 1868, 1894, and 1901, born at Pickhill, Yorkshire ca. 1831. He married at the Church of St. Mary the Virgin, Leake, Yorkshire 21 Dec. 1850,[64]

63. ANN SWAILES, a nurse in 1851, living in 1891, born at Osmotherley, Yorkshire 19 Dec. 1826.[65]

Sixth Generation

---

64. JOHN MIDDLETON, called a joiner and cabinet maker in his son's marriage record in 1838. He married at Wakefield, Yorkshire 5 Nov. 1806,[66]

65. ANNE BECKETT.

66. JOHN WARD, called a hatter in his daughter's marriage record in 1838. He married,[67]

67. MARGARET ——; perhaps the Margaret Ward, 50, living with Jane, 30, Sarah, 20, and Emma Ward, 13, in the Leeds West district of Yorkshire in 1841.[68]

68. JOHN ASQUITH, a cloth dresser in 1838 and 1841, born in Yorkshire ca. 1785 and died by 30 March 1851. He married,[69]

69. MARY ——, living 30 March 1851, born at Fairburn, Yorkshire ca. 1784.[70]

70. JOHN WARD = 66.
71. MARGARET —— = 67.

72. WILLIAM LUPTON, cloth merchant, born at Leeds, Yorkshire 8 June, baptized at the Church of St. Peter-at-Leeds 9 July 1777 and died 19 Aug. 1828. He married at the Church of St. Peter-at-Leeds 1 Aug. 1803,[71]

73. ANN DARNTON, born at Leeds 22 April, baptized at Call Lane Arian Congregation, Leeds 21 May 1784 and died at Gledhow Mount, Harehills Lane, Leeds 14 Aug. 1865; buried at St. John's Church, Round-hay, Yorkshire 19 Aug. 1865 aged 81.[72]

Of Ann (Darnton) Lupton, a family biographer noted that "Ann was only nineteen when she married. Not only was she a great standby to her husband and a joyful mother of his numerous children; but when left a widow at forty four with only two sons, Darnton and Arthur, old enough to carry on the business[,] she shouldered the responsibility successfully in most difficult times."[73]

Darnton Lupton served as Mayor of Leeds in 1844. Among William and Ann Lupton's great-grandchildren were Florence von Schunck, who married Albert Edward Kitson, 2nd Baron Airedale, and Barbara May Lupton, who married Sir Christopher Llewellyn Bullock, K.C.B., Permanent Undersecretary of the British Air Ministry 1931–36.

74. DR. THOMAS MICHAEL GREENHOW, F.R.C.S. (1843), sanitary reformer, born 5 July 1792, baptized at Christ Church, Tynemouth, Northumberland 20 May 1794 and died at Newton Hall, Chapel Aller-ton, Leeds, Yorkshire 25 Oct. 1881; buried at St. John's Church, Round-hay, Yorkshire 29 Oct. 1881 aged 89. He married, 2nd, at Leeds 31 May 1854, Anne Lupton, who was born 1 March, baptized at Call Lane Arian Congregation, Leeds 27 April 1812 and died 8 April 1905, daughter of William Lupton [No. 72] and Ann Darnton [No. 73]. He married, 1st, at St. Saviour's Church, Norwich, Norfolk 27 June 1820,[74]

75. ELIZABETH MARTINEAU, born 13 Aug., baptized at Octagon Presbyterian Church, Norwich 20 Sept. 1794 and died at Newcastle upon Tyne, Northumberland 10 Feb. 1850.[75]

Dr. Thomas Michael Greenhow was educated at the University of Edinburgh. For many years associated with the Newcastle Infirmary, he received an honorary M.D. from the new Durham University, where he was also appointed to a chair of Medical Ethics. In 1843, he was named one of the original three hundred Fellows of the Royal College of Surgeons. He is best remembered today for his fraught relationship with his sister-in-law, Harriet Martineau, whose ill health while his patient was alleviated by several courses of hypnosis. The ensuing correspondence—for both broadcast their views—enlivened breakfast tables from Leeds to London.[76]

76. REV. DR. RICHARD FRANCIS DAVIS, Rector of All Saints' Church, Worcester (1795), and Pendock, Worcestershire (1810), baptized at St. Helen's Church, Worcester, Worcestershire 23 Nov. 1766 and died at Pendock 25 Dec. 1844. He married at the Church of St. Martin-in-the-Fields, Westminster, Middlesex 22 Jan. 1799,[77]

77. SARAH STABLE, born 24 Oct., baptized at the Church of St. Clement Danes, London 24 Nov. 1778 and died 11 Jan. 1861.[78]

78. ROBERT HOBBES, attorney at law, gentleman in 1800, born at Wardington, Oxfordshire 15 July 1773 and died in 1817. He married at Holy Trinity Church, Stratford-upon-Avon, Warwickshire 16 Jan. 1800,[79]

79. ELIZABETH DAVENPORT ASHFORD, born 26 May, baptized at Holy Trinity Church 2 July 1777 and died in April 1825.[80]

80. THOMAS GLASSBOROW, a messenger in 1825, 1841, 1847, 1851, and 1860, called a fire office messenger in his widow's death record, born at London ca. 1796 (perhaps the Thomas Glassborow, son of Richard and Jane, baptized at St. Andrew's Church, Holborn, Middlesex 22 Sept. 1795) and died at 3 Nelson Terrace, Haggerston, Middlesex 29 Dec. 1860. He married at St. Mary's Church, Lambeth, Surrey 18 Feb. 1823,[81]

81. AMY HARVEY, born at Chesham, Surrey ca. 1788 and died at 3 Nelson Terrace 10 Jan. 1864.[82]

82. JOHN JOSEPH ABLETT, a farrier in 1825, 1841, and 1847, born ca. 1797 and died at 97 White Hart Street, Kennington, Surrey 20 Sept. 1847; buried at St. Mary's Church, Lambeth, Surrey 24 Sept. 1847. He married at St. Mary's Church 4 April 1820,[83]

83. CHARLOTTE GRAPES, born 10 Aug. 1799, baptized at the Church of St. Martin-in-the-Fields, Westminster, Middlesex 9 March 1800 and died at 97 White Hart Street 6 Jan. 1848; buried at St. Mary's Church 13 Jan. 1848.[84]

84. JOHN ELLIOTT of Cheshunt, Hertfordshire, called a coachman in his son's marriage record in 1843. He married,[85]

85. SARAH ——.

86. HENRY POWELL of Kennington, Surrey, called a jeweller in his daughter's marriage record in 1843. He married,[86]

87. HANNAH ——.

88-89. ——.

90. JOHN NEWBIGGING, baptized at Douglas, Lanarkshire 15 Sept. 1771. He married at Douglas 27 Nov. 1794,[87]

91. ANNE COVENTRY.

92. WILLIAM GEE, a victualler in 1841, gentleman in 1846, retired wine merchant in 1851, born at Knightsbridge ca. 1778 and died before 15 April 1852. He married at St. Mary's Church, Whitechapel, Middlesex 9 July 1810,[88]

93. ELIZABETH ROSE, died before 16 Dec. 1846.[89]

94. JAMES MARSHALL of Coventry, Warwickshire, called a gentleman in his daughter's marriage record in 1846. He married,[90]

95. MARY ——.[91]

96. JOHN GOLDSMITH, a carpenter in 1841, born in Kent ca. 1781 and died at Maidstone, Kent 7 June 1847 aged 66. He married,[92]

97. REBECCA WHEELER, born at Maidstone ca. 1796 and died at Church Street, Tovil, Maidstone 29 Dec. 1869 aged 74 [*sic*].[93]

98. JOHN JONES of Ware, Hertfordshire, called a labourer in his daughter's marriage record in 1850. He married,[94]

99. SARAH ——.

100. MICHAEL JAMES DORSETT, a labourer in 1841, called a labourer in his son's marriage record in 1845, baptized at St. Thomas' Church, Winchester, Hampshire 16 Aug. 1789. He married at All Saints' Church, Fulham, Middlesex 2 Sept. 1811,[95]

101. ANN HUGHES, living in 1841.

102. WILLIAM STANFORD POWELL, called a labourer in his daughter's marriage record in 1845. He married at All Saints' Church, Fulham, Middlesex 17 Dec. 1811,[96]

103. CHARLOTTE SMITH; a Charlotte Powell was buried at St. Nicholas' Church, Chiswick, Middlesex 13 March 1839 aged 48.[97]

104. BENJAMIN CHANDLER, died before 19 Feb. 1844. He married at St. Cyr's Church, Stonehouse, Gloucestershire 23 Feb. 1802,[98]

105. MARY BIRD, born in Gloucestershire ca. 1784 and died after 30 March 1851.[99]

106. JOHN JENKINGS of Upton upon Severn, Worcestershire, called a labourer in his daughter's marriage record in 1844. He married,[100]

107. SUSANNA ——.[101]

108. ?HARRY WHITE of Brewham, Somerset. He married,[102]

109. ?SARAH ——.

110. William Bowler of Iver, Buckinghamshire. He married,[103]
111. Ann ——.

112. James Harrison, a collier in 1841, coal miner in 1851, 1861, and 1866, miner in 1860, born at Byker, Northumberland ca. 1796 and died at Sherburn Hill, Durham 11 June 1866. He married,[104]
113. Jane ——, born at Byker ca. 1796 and died at Byker Hill 23 April 1845.[105]

114. Anthony Liddle, a pitman in 1838, coal miner in 1841 and 1851, called a miner in his daughter's marriage record in 1860, born at Chisle, Durham ca. 1817. He married at St. Laurence's Church, Pittington, Durham 18 Aug. 1838,[106]
115. Martha Stephenson, a washerwoman in 1871, charwoman in 1881, school caretaker in 1891, born at Penshaw, Durham ca. 1818 and died at Sherburn Hill, Durham 10 Oct. 1896.[107]

116. William Robson Hill, a mariner in 1838, 1844, 1851, and 1871, sailor in 1869, called a seaman (master) in the Merchant Service in his widow's death record in 1880, born at Shields, Durham ca. 1814 and died at 35 Tower Street, South Bishopwearmouth, Durham 17 March 1875. He married at Christ Church, Bishopwearmouth 27 Dec. 1838,[108]
117. Jane Dixon, born at Sunderland, Durham 19 Aug. 1815 and died at 20 Milbanke Rowe, South Bishopwearmouth 28 Feb. 1880.[109]

118. Thomas Hay Webster, a mariner in 1840, 1848, and 1861, called a sailor in his daughter's marriage record in 1869. He married at Christ Church, Bishopwearmouth, Durham 3 Sept. 1840,[110]
119. Elizabeth Golden, living in 1881, born at Bishopwearmouth ca. 1811.[111]

120. Thomas Temple, an alum work labourer in 1851, a miner in 1861, labourer in 1870 and 1871, born at Skelton, Yorkshire ca. 1797 and died at Guisborough, Yorkshire 28 Nov. 1880. He married,[112]

121. Elizabeth Park, born at Ellerby, Yorkshire 23 June 1806 and died at Guisborough 13 April 1880.[113]

122. David [sometimes Samuel] Stone, a labourer in 1845, 1854, 1857, and in his daughter's marriage record in 1870, rail labourer in 1851, excavator in 1851, ironstone labourer in 1861, called a foreman labourer in his widow's death record in 1909, baptized at St. Mary's Church, Sprowston, Norfolk 20 April 1817. He married at St. Remigius' Church, Hethersett, Norfolk 28 April 1845,[114]

123. Elizabeth Middleton, a cook in 1861, nurse in a miner's hospital in 1871, matron of an accidental hospital in 1881, born at Hethersett 10 Sept. 1820 and died at 1 Wilson Street, Guisborough, Yorkshire 5 May 1909.[115]

124. Joseph Myers of Holme or Pickhill, Yorkshire, called a labourer in his son's marriage record in 1850. He married,[116]

125. ——.

126. Robert Swales, a labourer in 1850, an agricultural labourer in 1851, 1861, and 1871, born at Appleton, Wirke, Yorkshire or Sowerby, Yorkshire ca. 1803. He married ca. 1826,[117]

127. Sarah Peacock, living in 1871, born at Great Smeaton, Yorkshire 25 Aug. 1799.[118]

Seventh Generation

128-143. ——.

144. ARTHUR LUPTON, born 20 Jan., baptized at the Church of St. Peter-at-Leeds, Yorkshire 14 Feb. 1747/48 and died at Leeds 7 July 1807. He married at Leeds 17 Nov. 1773,[119]

145. OLIVE RIDER, with a dowry of £5,000, born 6, baptized at the Call Lane Arian Congregation, Leeds 18 May 1753 and died 24 April 1803.[120]

The founder of the Lupton family fortune—William Lupton & Co., established in 1773, only ceased business in 1958—Arthur Lupton was educated in Frankfurt. (His elder brother established himself in Lisbon in the same period.) While in Germany Arthur befriended his schoolmaster's kinsman Johann Wolfgang von Goethe, who called him 'der junge Englander,' noting that "Lupton is a good felloe, a marry inventious fellow as I see in his letter, which is wroten with a spirit of jest, much laudably moderated by the respect he owes to his master." Goethe added that in 1764–65 he had "much intercourse with a young Englishman, who was a student at Herr Pfeil's pension. He had a good knowledge of his own language; I used to practice it with him, and thereby learned much about his Country and people. My sister was often a third party in our English conversation. And we both sought to acquire the amazing English pronunciation and therewith not only the special tones and sounds but also the very special peculiarities of our teacher, so that in the end it sounded odd enough when we seemed to be speaking together with one voice."

Dr. Charles Athelstane Lupton sums up the effect: "German with a good broad Yorkshire accent!"[121]

146. JOHN DARNTON, a tobacco merchant of the Headrow, Leeds, Yorkshire. He married,[122]

147. ANN ———.[123]

C. A. Lupton wrote of his forebear John Darnton that he was "a man of high principles and an active member of the Mill Hill congregation. It is said that he gave up business when he discovered the fraudulent practice of watering [tobacco] leaf and then selling by weight. There is a story that, when Dr. Williamson[,] a Congregational minister[,] was chidden by some strict member of his congregation for associating with this Arian [i.e., a member of another Protestant sect], he answered that as he was sure that he would never meet John Darnton in the next world he would do all he could to cultivate his society in this one."[124]

148. DR. EDWARD MARTIN GREENHOW, baptized at Stirling, Stirlingshire, Scotland 30 Dec. 1760 and died in 1835. He married at Christ Church, Tynemouth, Northumberland 5 Sept. 1786,[125]

149. MARY POWDITCH, baptized at Christ Church 16 Oct. 1765 and died in 1837.[126]

A nephew recalled that, as a young surgeon in Gibraltar in 1780, Dr. Greenhow "found the old and fatal system of dressing wounds in the tents, etc., in vogue, and was laughed to scorn for proposing to heal them by first intention. However, he persisted, and was obliged to obtain permission to do so by some superior authority. A failure was predicted. And when the first case, one of amputation, was opened out, all the surgeons and several of the military authorities were present. It was an unusually complete success. Most of the surgeons were Hanoverians, who were at the time much favoured by the Government. 'Dirty fellows' [Dr. Greenhow] used to call them."[127]

150. THOMAS MARTINEAU, manufacturer of camelots and bomba-zine, born 9 April, baptized at Octagon Presbyterian Church, Norwich, Norfolk 3 May 1764 and died 21 June 1826. He married at St. John's Church, Newcastle upon Tyne, Northumberland 29 Jan. 1793,[128]

151. ELIZABETH RANKIN, baptized at St. John's Church 6 Nov. 1771 and died at Highfield Road, Edgbaston, King's Norton, Worces-tershire 26 Aug. 1848.[129]

In addition to their eldest daughter Elizabeth [No. 75], Thomas and Elizabeth Martineau were the parents of Dr. Thomas Martineau (1795–1826); Henry (1797–1844), a wine importer; Robert (1798–1870), a brass founder; Rachel Ann (1800–1878), a schoolmistress in Liverpool; Harriet (1802–1876), the most famous member of the family; the Rev. James Martineau (1805–1900); and Ellen, wife of Dr. Alfred Higginson.[130]

James Martineau trained as an engineer before studying at Manchester College and entering the Unitarian ministry. After serving in Dublin and Liverpool, he joined the staff of Manchester College, first in York, later in London. He served as Principal of Manchester College from 1869 to 1885. He was "too broad-minded to belong to any school. Eclectic by nature, he gathered ideas from any source that appealed to his own intellectual and emotional character." A friend of Charles

Dickens, Sir Charles Lyall, and Alfred, Lord Tennyson, he received birthday greetings in 1883 from Robert Browning, James Russell Lowell, William James, and Joseph Chamberlain, prompting him to reply that "to be held of any account by the elite of those to whom I have habitually looked up . . . is an honour simply mysterious to me."[131]

Their great-great-nephew remarks that Elizabeth and James' sister, Harriet, "was a very different character." Frequently ill, hard of hearing and lacking a sense of taste or smell, she cannot have had an easy personality, but this only underlines her final triumph as one of the most influential social theorists of her time.

Her first essay was published in the *Unitarian Monthly Repository* in 1822. The stories in her *Illustrations of Political Economy* (published monthly in twenty-five parts from February 1832) "reinforced middle-class convictions and were welcomed accordingly." On her move to London in 1834, she became a celebrated resident of the city, renowned for her closely reasoned yet accessible works on political economy. Two years later Martineau paid a long visit to the United States, after which she published *Society in America* (1837), which "may be regarded as the best book among the vast outpouring of travel writing" of the period, with the exception of Alexis de Tocqueville's *Democracy in America*.

In the late 1830s, her health broke down, and she seemed likely to die of a slow-growing tumour; her brother-in-law, Dr. Thomas Michael Greenhow [No. 74] took on her case. (In this period, it is thought that Dickens used her as the model for Mrs. Jellyby in *Bleak House*.) Sessions with a number of different mesmerists seemed to help her symptoms, leading to much friction with the Greenhows. By the same token, the results were such that she was able to visit Palestine in 1846, and Martineau lived on until 1876.

In 1849–50, she published *The History of the Thirty Years' Peace*, which had "an acuteness and immediacy that support its claim to being, perhaps, her masterpiece. The tone of her editorial writing is confident, the style impeccable, the range astonishing."

Auguste Comte, who coined the term *sociology*, recommended Harriet Martineau's works on political economy in preference to his own. The author of more than fifty works, including a number of novels, Harriet Martineau summed up her own life as follows:

"Her original power was nothing more than was due to earnestness and intellectual clearness within a certain range. With small imaginative and suggestive powers, and therefore nothing approaching to genius, she could see clearly what she did see, and give a clear expression to what she had to say. In short, she could popularize while she could neither discover nor invent."[132]

152. THOMAS DAVIS, Mayor of Worcester in 1788, glove manufacturer, born in 1740 and died in 1820. He married at All Saints' Church, Newland, Gloucestershire 23 May 1765,[133]

153. JANE SLADEN, born in 1742 and died in 1812.[134]

154. WILLIAM STABLE, glover, born in March 1747 and died 11 April 1811. He married at St. Anne's Church, Soho, Westminster, Middlesex 19 Aug. 1772,[135]

155. JUDITH DORSETT, born 6, baptized at St. Anne's Church 22 Feb. 1756 and died at 34 Tything Street, Worcester, Worcestershire 30 Dec. 1846 aged 90.[136]

156. JONATHAN HOBBS, born at Gloucester in 1736 and died 27 Sept. 1787; buried at Sherbourne, near Warwick. He married at New Church, Birmingham, Warwickshire 3 Feb. 1761,[137]

157. KATHERINE WARD, born 16 June 1739 and died at Coventry, Warwickshire 24 March 1811; buried at Sherbourne 28 March 1811.[138]

158. THOMAS ASHFORD, saddler's bridle cutter and ironmonger, born in 1731 and died at Stratford-upon-Avon, Warwickshire 12 Feb. 1797. He married at Bardwell, Suffolk 8 June 1775,[139]

159. SARAH DAVENPORT, baptized in 1741 and died at Stratford-upon-Avon 24 Jan. 1805.[140]

160. ?RICHARD GLASSBORROW of Holborn, Middlesex. He married,[141]
161. ?JANE ——.

162–165. ——.

166. JOSEPH GRAPES, baptized at the Church of St. Giles Cripplegate, London 16 March 1760 and died at Bishopsgate, London 1 July 1837. He married at St. Anne's Church, Soho, Westminster, Middlesex 17 Feb. 1795,[142]
167. JANE CELLSON.

168–179. ——.

180. JAMES NEWBIGGING, baptized at Lesmahagow, Lanarkshire 19 Feb. 1727. He married,[143]
181. JANET MUIR.

182–199. ——.

200. JAMES DORSETT. He married,[144]
201. SARAH ——.

202. ?CHARLES HUGHES. He married,[145]
203. ?ANN ——.

204–227. ——.

228. James Liddell, called a pitman in his son's marriage record in 1838. He married,[146]
229. ——.

230. John Stephenson, called a pitman in his daughter's marriage record in 1838. He married,[147]
231. ——.

232. William Hill, called a mariner in his son's marriage record in 1838. He married,[148]
233. ——.

234. Charles Dixon, a mariner in 1838 and 1841, born in Durham ca. 1793. He married at Bishopwearmouth, Durham 7 May 1810,[149]
235. Isabella Stafford, living in 1841, baptized at Sunderland, Durham 12 Jan. 1794.[150]

236. Thomas Hay Webster, called a grocer in his son's marriage record in 1840. He married,[151]
237. ——.

238. William Golden, called a mariner in his daughter's marriage record in 1840. He married,
239. Jane ——, born at Bishopwearmouth, Durham ca. 1792 and died 10 or 11 West Trimdon Street, Sunderland, Durham 23 Dec. 1865.[152]

240–241. ——.

242.   JOSEPH PARK. He married at St. Oswald's Church, Lythe, Yorkshire 30 March 1793,[153]

243. ELIZABETH DALE.

244.   SAMUEL STONE, an agricultural labourer in 1841, a labourer in 1845, born at Rackheath, Norfolk 16, baptized at South Acre, Norfolk 20 Sept. 1789. He married at St. Mary's Church, Sprowston, Norfolk 29 Nov. 1813,[154]

245. MARY GERMANY, died by 1841.[155]

246.   JOSEPH MIDDLETON, an agricultural labourer in 1841, a labourer in his daughter's marriage record in 1845, born in Norfolk ca. 1781. He married at Hethersett, Norfolk 9 Aug. 1802,[156]

247.   ELIZABETH BANYARD, born in Norfolk ca. 1786.

248–253. ——.

254.   THOMAS PEACOCK, born in 1760 and died at Hawnby, Yorkshire 28 March 1822. He married at Hawnby 25 Jan. 1786,[157]

255.   ANN ATKINSON, baptized at Bilsdale Midcable, Yorkshire 28 Sept. 1766.[158]

Eighth Generation

256–287. ——.

288. William Lupton, yeoman of Seacroft in the parish of Whit-kirk or Hickson, near Leeds, Yorkshire, "a gentleman greatly respected by all who knew him for his upright, uniform and affable behaviour in every station of his life," born 2, baptized at the Church of St. Peter-at-Leeds 18 Sept. 1700 and buried there 5 March 1771. He married at the Church of St. Peter-at-Leeds 4 Feb. 1730,[159]

289. Mary Higson, born 15, baptized at the Church of St. Peter-at-Leeds 22 June 1715 and buried there 31 Dec. 1760.[160]

290. David Rider, a clothworker "with considerable property" in Leeds, born in 1716 and died in 1801. He married at St. Mary's Church, Whitkirk, Yorkshire 3 Oct. 1751,[161]

291. Olive Arey, baptized at Call Lane Arian Congregation, Leeds, Yorkshire 17 Feb. 1728 and died ca. 6 May 1753.[162]

292. ?John Darnton of Leeds, Yorkshire. He married,
293. ——.

294–295. ——.

296. **CAPTAIN MICHAEL GREENHOW** of Kirkby Hill, near Richmond, Yorkshire, Commandant of Stirling Castle in 1760, baptized at Hutton Magna, Yorkshire 22 May 1718. He married, 1st, at the Church of St. Bartholomew the Less, London 31 Aug. 1740, Martha Archambo, who was born 13 and baptized at the Church of St. Martin-in-the-Fields, Westminster, Middlesex 15 Feb. 1725, daughter of Peter Archambo and Elizabeth ———. He married, 2nd, before 26 Aug. 1752,[163]

297. **ELIZABETH WOODWARD.**

298. **THOMAS POWDITCH.** He married at St. Hilda's Church, South Shields, Durham 4 May 1750,[164]

299. **MARGARET BELL.**

300. **DR. DAVID MARTINEAU,** "eminently distinguished as a surgeon, as a man of most amiable manners, and as the best of fathers," baptized at Octagon Presbyterian Church, Norwich, Norfolk 21 Nov. 1726 and died 19 Nov. 1768; buried in the Church of St. Mary the Less, Norwich. He married at the Church of St. George Colegate, Norwich 21 Jan. 1751/52,[165]

301. **SARAH MEADOWS,** "eminently distinguished for sound judgment, warm affection, and fervent piety," born 9, baptized at the Church of St. George Colegate 24 Feb. 1725 and died 26 Nov. 1800; buried in the Church of St. Mary the Less.[166]

> Anna Letitia Barbould's "On the Death of Mrs. Martineau" begins:
>
> *Ye who around this venerated bier*
> *In pious anguish pour the tender tear,*
> *Mourn not!—'Tis Virtue's triumph, Nature's doom,*
> *When honoured Age, slow bending to the tomb,*
> *Earth's vain enjoyments past, her transient woes,*
> *Tastes the long sabbath of well-earned repose.*

> It ends with the lines:
> *—For me, as over the frequent grave I bend,*
> *And pensive down the vale of years descend;*
> *Companions, Parents, Kindred call to mourn,*
> *Dropt from my side, or from my bosom torn;*
> *A boding voice, methinks, in Fancy's ear*
> *Speaks from the tomb, and cries "Thy friends are here!"*[167]

302. ROBERT RANKIN, sugar refiner in Newcastle upon Tyne (perhaps the Robert Rankin, son of Robert, born 21 Oct. and baptized at Groat Market Meeting, Newcastle 14 Nov. 1742). He married at St. Mary's Church, Whickham, Durham 9 July 1767,[168]

303. ANN COLE, born ca. 1749 (perhaps the Ann Cole, daughter of John, baptized at St. John's Church, Newcastle 9 March 1750) and died at Newcastle 7 Nov. 1840 aged 91.[169]

304–307. ——.

308. JOHN STABLE. He married 9 July 1745,[170]
309. SARAH JOYNER.

310. BENJAMIN DORSETT. He married at St. Benet's Church, Paul's Wharf, London 23 Feb. 1746,[171]
311. ELIZABETH LOWEN.

312. THOMAS HOBBS, architect, buried at Gloucester, Gloucestershire. He married,[172]
313. MARY MATTHEWS, whose "brother was a great favourite of Oliver Cromwell [*sic*], and was said to be the first swordsman in Europe."[173]

314. John Ward, born in 1707 and died in 1765. He married,[174]
315. Ann Billingsby, born in 1709 and died in 1782.

316–317. ——.

318. William Davenport, born in 1713 and died in 1798. He married,[175]
319. Elizabeth Marshall, born in 1714 and died in 1799.

320–331. ——.

332. Joseph Grapes. He married at the Church of St. Clement Danes, London 16 April 1759,[176]
333. Ann Hutton.

334–359. ——.

360. James Newbigging, born ca. 1697. He married at Lesmahagow, Lanarkshire 29 Oct. 1726,[177]
361. Grissel Watson.

362–469. ——.

470. Jonas Stafford of Sunderland, Durham. He married,[178]
471. Jane Matthews.

472–487. ——.

488. EDWARD STONE of South Acre, Norfolk. He married before 20 Sept. 1789,[179]

489. ELIZABETH WOODS.

490–509. ——.

510. WILLIAM ATKINSON, born ca. 1727 and died at Hawnby, Yorkshire 16 Feb. 1809. He married at Kirby, Cleveland, Yorkshire 2 June 1760,[180]

511. ELIZABETH DOUGLAS, born at Hawnby 17 Nov. 1734 and died there 13 March 1819.[181]

Ninth Generation

512–575. ——.

576. FRANCIS LUPTON, "a man of some education and complete integrity," clerk of the Church of St. Peter-at-Leeds 1694–1717, born at Leeds, Yorkshire in 1658 (perhaps the Francis Lupton, son of Thomas, baptized at Pateley Bridge, Yorkshire 3 May 1657) and buried at the Church of St. Peter-at-Leeds 28 Aug. 1717. He married at the Church of St. John the Baptist, Adel, Yorkshire 8 Nov. 1688,[182]

577. ESTHER MIDGELEY, baptized at the Church of St. John the Baptist 28 April 1669 and buried at the Church of St. Peter-at-Leeds 30 July 1726.[183]

578. ARTHUR HIGSON of Giggleswick and Leeds, Yorkshire. He married,[184]

579. ——.

580. JONATHAN RIDER, born in 1684 and died in 1758. He married at the Church of St. Peter-at-Leeds, Yorkshire 7 Jan. 1709,[185]

581. MARY BARWICK, born 26 July, baptized at the Church of St. Peter-at-Leeds 22 Aug. 1691 and died in 1758.[186]

582. WILLIAM AREY, born and baptized at the Church of St. Peter-at-Leeds, Yorkshire 9 June 1692 and died in 1736. He married in 1722,[187]

583. Olive Lister, born in 1698 (perhaps the Olove Lister, daughter of Thomas, born 24 March 1696 and baptized at Mill Hill Chapel, Leeds 18 April 1697) and died in 1739.[188]

584–591. ——.

592. Michael Greenhow, baptized at Kirkby Ravensworth, Yorkshire 8 Feb. 1679 and buried at Hutton Magna, Yorkshire 8 Sept. 1747. He married,[189]

593. Sarah Heslop, born at Richmond, Yorkshire in 1682 (perhaps the Sarah Heslop, daughter of Christopher, baptized at Grinton, near Richmond, 28 Aug. 1687).[190]

594–595. ——.

596. Thomas Powditch. He married at Lowestoft, Suffolk 29 March 1725,[191]

597. Grace Kitteredge.

598–599. ——.

600. Dr. David Martineau, "a skilful Surgeon," born and baptized at the Church of St. Michael-at-Plea, Norwich, Norfolk 10 April 1697 and died 29 May 1729; buried in the Church of St. Mary the Less, Norwich. He married at the Church of St. George Tombland, Norwich 22 Aug. 1721,[192]

601. Elizabeth Finch, baptized at the Church of St. George Tombland 16 Aug. 1702 and died in 1748; buried in the Church of St. Mary the Less. She married, 2nd, at Bramerton, Norfolk 14 July 1738, Dr. Kirvin Wright, whose will was dated 2 April 1750, son of Kirvin Wright and Sarah Meadows, daughter of the Rev. John Meadows [No. 1204] and Sarah Fairfax [No. 1205].[193]

602. Philip Meadows, Sheriff of Norwich in 1724, an Alderman in 1724, Mayor in 1734, merchant, born 17 July 1679 and died 11 Feb. 1752. He married before 13 May 1718,[194]

603. Margaret Hall, baptized at the Church of St. George Colegate, Norwich, Norfolk 28 Jan. 1691 and died 22 Feb. 1765.[195]

604. ?Robert Rankin. He married at St. Mary's Church, Gateshead, Durham 14 Sept. 1734,[196]

605. ?Ann Burdon.

606. ?John Cole of Whickham, Durham. He married,

607. ——.

608–615. ——.

616. William Stable of Lincoln's Inn Fields, Westminster, Middlesex, will dated 2 and proved 24 March 1784. He married,[197]

617. ——.

618. Lorenzo Joyner. He married at Elstree, Hertfordshire 31 Jan. 1724,[198]

619. Jane Montague, perhaps the Jane Montague, daughter of George and Susanna, baptized at Elstree 22 Nov. 1705.[199]

620–623. ——.

624. Charles Hobbs, born in 1596 and died in 1700; buried in the Cathedral Churchyard at Gloucester, Gloucestershire. He married,[200]

625. ——.

626–627. ——.

628. William Ward, a farmer in the parish of Yardley, Worcestershire. He married,[201]
629. Sarah Gibbons.

630–635. ——.

636. William Davenport, probably the "William Danport" baptized at St. Giles' Church, Reading, Berkshire 19 Oct. 1682 and buried at St. Laurence's Church, Reading 24 April 1723. He married at All Saints' Church, Swallowfield, Berkshire 11 June 1707,[202]
637. Grace Alloway, baptized at Mapledurham, Oxfordshire 7 March 1680/81 and buried at St. Laurence's Church 19 Oct. 1757. She married, 2nd, 15 May 1726, Peter Broach of Sonning, near Reading.[203]

638–719. ——.

720. James Newbigging. He married,[204]
721. Janet Allan.

722. Thomas Watson. He married at Lesmahagow, Lanarkshire 23 April 1708,[205]
723. Jean Weir.

724–1021. ——.

1022. John Douglas, born ca. 1700 and died at Kirby, Cleveland, Yorkshire 5 May 1722 [*sic*]. He married at Kirby 7 April 1724,[206]
1023. Ann Proud, born at Kirby 15 March 1697/98 and died there 26 Nov. 1754.[207]

Tenth Generation

1024–1153. ——.

1154. RALPH MIDGELEY, yeoman of Breary, baptized at the Church of St. John the Baptist, Adel, Yorkshire 18 Feb. 1621 (N.S.) and buried there 12 July 1694 aged 65 [*sic*]. He married,[208]

1155. FRANCES BURNISTON, baptized at the Church of St. Peter-at-Leeds, Yorkshire 5 Nov. 1629 and died 21 Feb. 1706; buried at the Church of St. John the Baptist.[209]

1156–1159. ——.

1160. ROBERT RIDER, born in 1633. He married,[210]
1161. ——.

1162. PETER BARWICK of Leeds, Yorkshire. He married,[211]
1163. ——.

1164. WILLIAM AREY of Leeds, Yorkshire. He married,[212]
1165. SARAH ——.

1166. ?THOMAS LISTER of Leeds, Yorkshire. He married,[213]
1167. ——.

1168–1183. ——.

1184. THOMAS GREENHOW of Kirkby Ravensworth, Yorkshire. He married,[214]
    1185. ——.

1186. ?CHRISTOPHER HESLOP of Grinton, Yorkshire. He perhaps married at Forcett, Yorkshire 4 May 1680,[215]
    1187. ?MARY LIGHTFOOT.

1188–1199. ——.

1200. DR. GASTON MARTINEAU, surgeon, born at Bergerac, Dordogne ca. 1654. He fled France in 1685 and was naturalized in England 21 March 1688. His will was dated 12 Aug. and proved 23 Nov. 1726. He married at Norwich, Norfolk 26 Sept. 1693,[216]
    1201. MARY PIERRE.

The nineteenth-century Martineau memorial tablet at the Church of St. Mary the Less in Norwich reads:

In memory of
[G]ASTON MARTINEAU, of Dieppe, Surgeon,
Who left France on the revocation of the
Edict of Nantes in 1685
and settled at Norwich in 1695.

And of DAVID MARTINEAU, his Son,
Likewise a skilful Surgeon.
He married ELIZABETH FINCH by whom he left
one son and two daughters,
and died 29th May 1729, aged 32.

Also of his son,
DAVID MARTINEAU,
born in 1726,
and who died 19th November, 1768, aged 42,
eminent in his profession as a Surgeon.
He married SARAH, second daughter of PHILIP
MEADOWS, Esq.
She was distinguished for sound judgment, warm affection,
and fervent piety,
and died 26th November 1800, aged 74.

The above were all buried in this church.
DAVID and SARAH MARTINEAU had five sons:
PHILIP MEADOWS, DAVID, PETER FINCH, JOHN,
and THOMAS,
From whom have descended
The numerous family of MARTINEAU.
ERECTED 1856.[217]

1202. REV. PETER FINCH, minister of the English Presbyterian Chapel, Norwich, born and baptized at St. Mary's Church, Walton on the Hill, Lancashire 6 Oct. 1661 and died 6 Oct. 1754; buried at the Church of St. Peter Mancroft, Norwich, Norfolk. He married (perhaps the Peter Finch who married Elizabeth Macconi at the Church of St. John the Baptist, Lakenham, Norfolk 23 Feb. 1692),[218]

1203. ELIZABETH MACKERELL, baptized at the Church of St. Peter Mancroft 12 Aug. 1671.[219]

1204. REV. JOHN MEADOWS, Vicar of Ousden, Suffolk (ejected in 1662), born at Chattisham, Suffolk 7, baptized at St. Mary's Church, Coddenham, Suffolk 29 April 1622 and buried at Stowmarket, near Bury St. Edmunds, Suffolk 1 March 1697. He married, 1st, before 26 Aug. 1653, Ann Rant, who died about 1670, daughter of Roger Rant of Swaffham Prior, Cambridgeshire. He married, 3rd, Anna or Hannah

Beaumont, who died in 1707, daughter of John Beaumont. He married, 2nd, ca. 1675,[220]

1205. Sarah Fairfax, born in 1654 and died in Feb. 1687/88; buried at Stowmarket.[221]

1206. John Hall, Sheriff of Norwich in 1693, Mayor in 1701 and 1719, born in 1653 and died 14 April 1729. He married,[222]

1207. Margaret Lumbe, born in 1652 and died 12 May 1722.

1208–1237. ——.

1238. ?George Montague of Elstree, Hertfordshire. He married before 6 March 1691,[223]

1239. ?Susanna ——.

1240–1271. ——.

1272. ?Laurence Davenport, perhaps married at the Church of St. Mary le Bone, Westminster, Middlesex 22 Aug. 1681,[224]

1273. ?Elizabeth Lewis, buried at St. Laurence's Church, Reading, Berkshire 29 Oct. 1712.[225]

1274. Richard Alloway, buried at Mapledurham, Oxfordshire 10 March 1713. He married,[226]

1275. Jane ——, buried at Mapledurham 19 Jan. 1711.[227]

1276–1445. ——.

1446. George Muir of Lesmahagow, Lanarkshire. He married,[228]

1447. ——.

1448-2045. ——.

2046. THOMAS PROUD, died at Kirby, Cleveland, Yorkshire 6 Aug. 1705. He married ca. 1685,[229]

2047. ELIZABETH DUNN, born ca. 1660 and died at Yarm, Yorkshire in Oct. 1719.

Eleventh Generation

2048–2307. ——.

2308. ROBERT MIDGELEY of Breary in Adel, Yorkshire. He married,[230]
2309. MARY SMITH of London.[231]

2310. GEORGE BURNISTON of Potternewton, Yorkshire. He married,[232]
2311. ——.

2312–2399. ——.

2400. ELIE MARTINEAU of Bergerac, Dordogne. He married,[233]
2401. MARGUERITE BARBESSON.

2402. GUILLAUME PIERRE, a Huguenot refugee naturalized in England 20 March 1686/87. He married,[234]
2403. MARIE JOURDAIN.

2404. REV. HENRY FINCH, Vicar of Walton on the Hill, Lancashire (ejected 1662), nonconformist minister of Birch Hall, Lancashire, baptized at Standish, Lancashire 8 Sept. 1633 and died 13 Nov. 1704; buried at the Collegiate Church, Manchester, Lancashire 16 Nov. 1704. He married at St. Elphin's Church, Warrington, Lancashire 11 Oct. 1659,[235]
2405. MARY HAMMOND.

2406. John Mackerell, Alderman of Norwich, born in 1643 and died 16 March 1723; buried at the Church of St. Peter Mancroft, Norwich, Norfolk 22 March 1723. He married before 12 Aug. 1671,[236]

2407. Anne Browne, baptized at the Church of St. Peter Mancroft 6 Jan. 1647 and buried there 10 Jan. 1722.[237]

2408. Daniel Meadows, born at Rushmere, Suffolk in 1577 and died 7 September 1651 aged 74; buried at Chattisham, Suffolk. He married,[238]

2409. Elizabeth Smith, died at Stowmarket, Suffolk in 1678.[239]

2410. Rev. Benjamin Fairfax, Curate of Halesworth, Suffolk, died in 1708. He married, 2nd, in 1670, ———. He married, 1st,[240]

2411. Bridget Stringer.

2412–2413. ———.

2414. Edward Lumbe. He married,[241]

2415. ———.

Edward Lumbe's eldest son, Henry, was the father of Sir Thomas Lumbe (father of the Countess of Lauderdale). "This Sir Thomas and his youngest brother John were the first who introduced into this kingdom organized silk (a trade before confined to the Italians), and they erected the famous mills at Danby. John was supposed to have been, in consequence, poisoned by some Italians, and Sir Thomas had 14,000 *l.* [£14,000] granted him by Parliament, 5 Geo. II [1732/33]."[242]

2416–4091. ———.

4092. THOMAS PROUD, buried at All Saints' Church, Hawnby, Yorkshire 18 Jan. 1689. He married,[243]

4093. MARY ——, died at Hawnby in Dec. 1694.

4094–4095. ——.

Twelfth Generation

4096–4615. ——.

4616. JOHN MIDGELEY. He married,[244]
4617. ——.

4618–4799. ——.

4800. DENIS MARTINEAU, living 4 May 1651. He married,[245]
4801. B—— BOUHEREAU, living as a widow aged about 80 in 1685.

4802–4805. ——.

4806. NICHOLAS JOURDAIN. He married,[246]
4807. ——.

4808. PETER FINCH. He married,[247]
4809. KATHERINE ——.

4810–4811. ——.

4812. JOHN MACKERELL, weaver, born 13, baptized at St. Andrew's Church, Norwich, Norfolk 28 July 1618 and buried at St. Gregory's Church, Norwich 27 Jan. 1659/60. He married there 4 Feb. 1642,[248]

4813. Abigail Anton, sister of Peter Anton, buried at St. Gregory's Church 10 Oct. 1698.[249]

4814. Elias Browne, Sheriff of Norwich in 1660, goldsmith, baptized at the Church of St. George Tombland, Norwich, Norfolk 11 Sept. 1605 and died 12 Oct. 1660; buried at the Church of St. Peter Mancroft, Norwich. He married,[250]
4815. Ann ——.

4816. William Meadows, born in 1530. He married,[251]
4817. Agnes ——, died in 1588.

4818. Robert Smith of Wickham Market, Suffolk. He married,[252]
4819. ——.

4820. Rev. Benjamin Fairfax, Rector of Rumburgh, Suffolk, ejected 1662, born in 1592 and died in 1675 or 1676. He married,[253]
4821. Sarah Galliard.

4822. Walter Stringer of Chester, Cheshire. He married,[254]
4823. ——.

4824–4827. ——.

4828. Thomas Lumbe. He married,[255]
4829. ——.

4830–8191. ——.

Thirteenth Generation

8192–9231. ——.

9232. RICHARD MIDGELEY of Breary in Adel, Yorkshire. He married,[256]
9233. ——.

9234–9623. ——.

9624. ?NICHOLAIS MAKEREEL, a native of the Netherlands living in Norwich, Norfolk in 1621. He married before 28 July 1618,[257]
9625. ABIGAIL ——.

9626. JOHN BROWNE of Norwich, Norfolk. He married,[258]
9627. ——.

9628–9639. ——.

9640. JOHN FAIRFAX, master of the great Hospital of Holme St. Mary, Norwich, Norfolk in 1609, died in 1614. His will was dated 18 Feb. 1614 and proved at Norwich 17 March 1614. He married at the Church of St. Michael Coslany, Norwich 10 Oct. 1580,[259]
9641. MARY BIRCH. Her will was dated 13 April 1615 and proved at Norwich 10 June 1615.[260]

9642. ROGER GALLIARD of Wreningham and Ashwellthorpe, Norfolk, died in 1672. He married,[261]

9643. JOAN ——.

9644–16383. ——.

Fourteenth Generation

16384–18463. ——.

18464. EDWARD MIDGELY of Midgley, near Halifax, Yorkshire. He married,[262]
    18465. ——.

18466–19279. ——.

19280. WILLIAM FAIRFAX of Bury St. Edmunds, Suffolk. According to Joseph Foster, William was a younger twin of his brother Sir Nicholas Fairfax, who was aged 22 in 1521, although if William was born about 1499 he did not get married for the first time until he was 42. He was buried at Walsingham, Norfolk 12 Dec. 1588. He married, first, at St. Mary's Church, Bury St. Edmunds 26 Oct. 1541, Anne Baker, and second, Katherine Tanfield, daughter of Robert Tanfield. William had four sons – John, William, Thomas, and Stephen – although their birth order, and their mother, has not been determined.[263]
    19281. ——.

19282. GEORGE BIRCH, Sheriff of Norwich in 1604, Mayor in 1621, grocer and apothecary, died in 1632. He married,[264]
    19283. ——.

19284–32767. ——.

Fifteenth Generation

32768–38559. ——.

38560. SIR THOMAS FAIRFAX of Walton and Gilling, Yorkshire, born ca. 1476 and died 1 Dec. 1520. His will was dated 26 Nov. 1520 and proved 20 Jan. 1520/21. He married,[265]
38561. AGNES GASCOIGNE.

38562–65535. ——.

Charts

I.
Edward III
and His Family

THE EARLS OF KENT

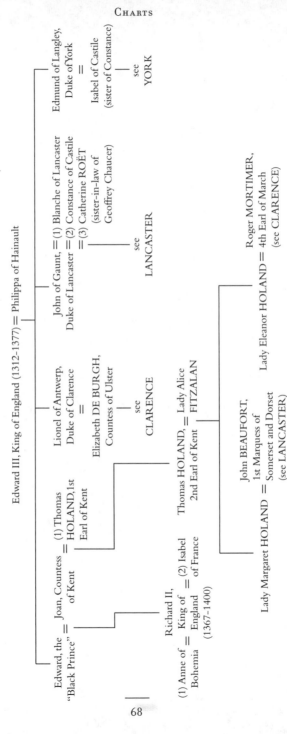

Edward III, King of England (1312-1377) = Philippa of Hainault

Edward, the "Black Prince" = Joan, Countess of Kent = (1) Thomas HOLAND, 1st Earl of Kent

Richard II, King of England (1367-1400) = (1) Anne of Bohemia = (2) Isabel of France

Thomas HOLAND, 2nd Earl of Kent = Lady Alice FITZALAN

Lady Margaret HOLAND = John BEAUFORT, 1st Marquess of Somerset and Dorset (see LANCASTER)

Lady Eleanor HOLAND = Roger MORTIMER, 4th Earl of March (see CLARENCE)

Lionel of Antwerp, Duke of Clarence = Elizabeth DE BURGH, Countess of Ulster

see CLARENCE

John of Gaunt, Duke of Lancaster = (1) Blanche of Lancaster = (2) Constance of Castile = (3) Catherine ROËT (sister-in-law of Geoffrey Chaucer)

see LANCASTER

Edmund of Langley, Duke of York = Isabel of Castile (sister of Constance)

see YORK

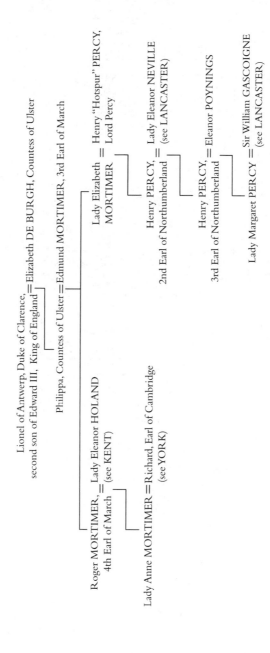

THE DUKE OF CLARENCE

Lionel of Antwerp, Duke of Clarence,
second son of Edward III, King of England = Elizabeth DE BURGH, Countess of Ulster

Philippa, Countess of Ulster = Edmund MORTIMER, 3rd Earl of March

Roger MORTIMER, = Lady Eleanor HOLAND
4th Earl of March   (see KENT)

Lady Anne MORTIMER = Richard, Earl of Cambridge
                                          (see YORK)

Lady Elizabeth = Henry "Hotspur" PERCY,
MORTIMER   Lord Percy

Henry PERCY, = Lady Eleanor NEVILLE
2nd Earl of Northumberland   (see LANCASTER)

Henry PERCY, = Eleanor POYNINGS
3rd Earl of Northumberland

Lady Margaret PERCY = Sir William GASCOIGNE
                                       (see LANCASTER)

THE DUKE OF LANCASTER

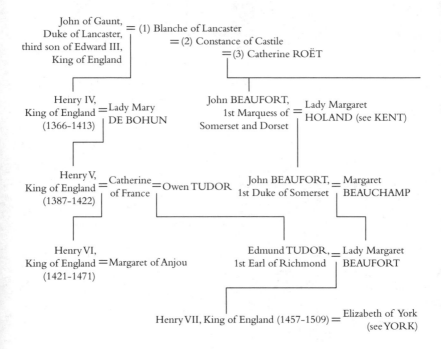

John of Gaunt, Duke of Lancaster, third son of Edward III, King of England = (1) Blanche of Lancaster
= (2) Constance of Castile
= (3) Catherine ROËT

Henry IV, King of England (1366-1413) = Lady Mary DE BOHUN

John BEAUFORT, 1st Marquess of Somerset and Dorset = Lady Margaret HOLAND (see KENT)

Henry V, King of England (1387-1422) = Catherine of France = Owen TUDOR

John BEAUFORT, 1st Duke of Somerset = Margaret BEAUCHAMP

Henry VI, King of England (1421-1471) = Margaret of Anjou

Edmund TUDOR, 1st Earl of Richmond = Lady Margaret BEAUFORT

Henry VII, King of England (1457-1509) = Elizabeth of York (see YORK)

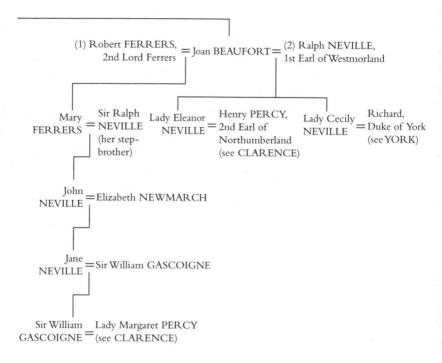

THE DUKES OF YORK

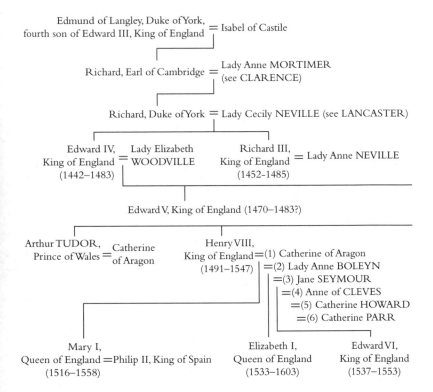

Edmund of Langley, Duke of York,
fourth son of Edward III, King of England = Isabel of Castile

Richard, Earl of Cambridge = Lady Anne MORTIMER
(see CLARENCE)

Richard, Duke of York = Lady Cecily NEVILLE (see LANCASTER)

Edward IV,
King of England = Lady Elizabeth
WOODVILLE
(1442–1483)

Richard III,
King of England = Lady Anne NEVILLE
(1452-1485)

Edward V, King of England (1470–1483?)

Arthur TUDOR,
Prince of Wales = Catherine
of Aragon

Henry VIII,
King of England = (1) Catherine of Aragon
(1491–1547) = (2) Lady Anne BOLEYN
= (3) Jane SEYMOUR
= (4) Anne of CLEVES
= (5) Catherine HOWARD
= (6) Catherine PARR

Mary I,
Queen of England = Philip II, King of Spain
(1516–1558)

Elizabeth I,
Queen of England
(1533–1603)

Edward VI,
King of England
(1537–1553)

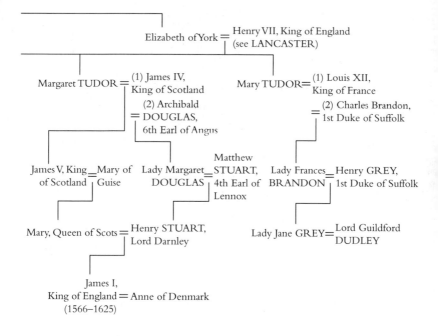

Elizabeth of York = Henry VII, King of England
(see LANCASTER)

Margaret TUDOR = (1) James IV, King of Scotland
= (2) Archibald DOUGLAS, 6th Earl of Angus

Mary TUDOR = (1) Louis XII, King of France
= (2) Charles Brandon, 1st Duke of Suffolk

James V, King of Scotland _ Mary of Guise

Lady Margaret DOUGLAS _ Matthew STUART, 4th Earl of Lennox

Lady Frances BRANDON = Henry GREY, 1st Duke of Suffolk

Mary, Queen of Scots = Henry STUART, Lord Darnley

Lady Jane GREY = Lord Guildford DUDLEY

James I, King of England = Anne of Denmark
(1566–1625)

II.
Connections to
American Immigrants

BLADEN, READE, SALTONSTALL, and MAULEVERER

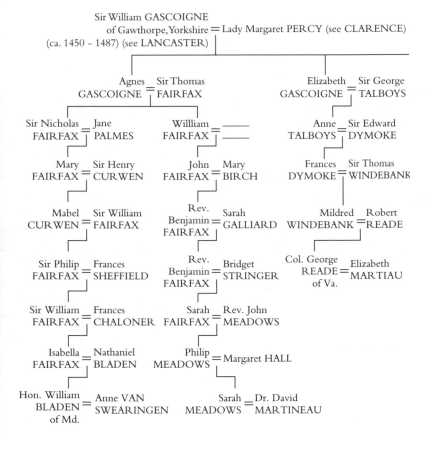

Sir William GASCOIGNE
of Gawthorpe, Yorkshire = Lady Margaret PERCY (see CLARENCE)
(ca. 1450 - 1487) (see LANCASTER)

Agnes _ Sir Thomas
GASCOIGNE = FAIRFAX

Elizabeth _ Sir George
GASCOIGNE = TALBOYS

Sir Nicholas _ Jane
FAIRFAX = PALMES

Willliam _ ——
FAIRFAX = ——

Anne _ Sir Edward
TALBOYS = DYMOKE

Mary _ Sir Henry
FAIRFAX = CURWEN

John _ Mary
FAIRFAX = BIRCH

Frances _ Sir Thomas
DYMOKE = WINDEBANK

Mabel _ Sir William
CURWEN = FAIRFAX

Rev.
Benjamin _ Sarah
FAIRFAX = GALLIARD

Mildred   Robert
WINDEBANK = READE

Sir Philip _ Frances
FAIRFAX = SHEFFIELD

Rev.
Benjamin _ Bridget
FAIRFAX = STRINGER

Col. George _ Elizabeth
READE = MARTIAU
of Va.

Sir William _ Frances
FAIRFAX = CHALONER

Sarah _ Rev. John
FAIRFAX = MEADOWS

Isabella _ Nathaniel
FAIRFAX = BLADEN

Philip _ Margaret HALL
MEADOWS =

Hon. William _ Anne VAN
BLADEN = SWEARINGEN
of Md.

Sarah _ Dr. David
MEADOWS = MARTINEAU

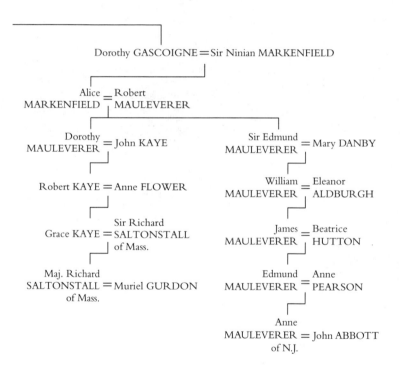

Dorothy GASCOIGNE = Sir Ninian MARKENFIELD

Alice ─ Robert
MARKENFIELD ┬ MAULEVERER

Dorothy = John KAYE
MAULEVERER

Robert KAYE = Anne FLOWER

Grace KAYE = Sir Richard
SALTONSTALL
of Mass.

Maj. Richard
SALTONSTALL = Muriel GURDON
of Mass.

Sir Edmund ─ Mary DANBY
MAULEVERER =

William ─ Eleanor
MAULEVERER ═ ALDBURGH

James ─ Beatrice
MAULEVERER ═ HUTTON

Edmund ─ Anne
MAULEVERER ═ PEARSON

Anne
MAULEVERER = John ABBOTT
of N.J.

DIGGES, HORSMANDEN, CULPEPER, CODD, and ARNOLD

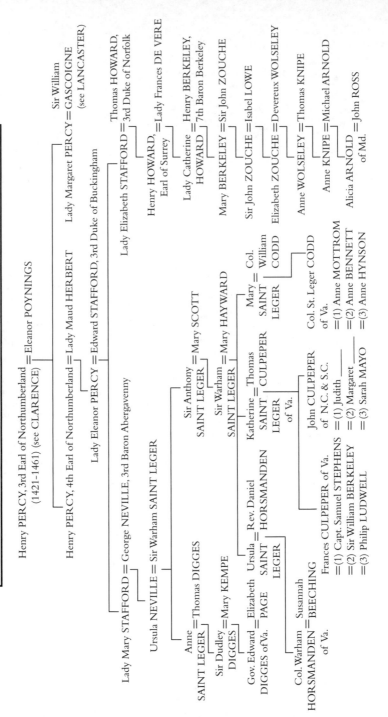

CARLETON

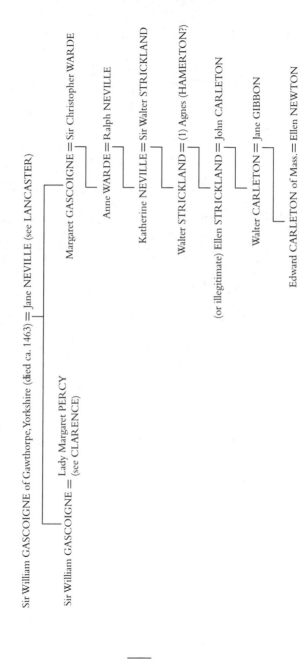

Sir William GASCOIGNE of Gawthorpe, Yorkshire (died ca. 1463) = Jane NEVILLE (see LANCASTER)

Sir William GASCOIGNE = Lady Margaret PERCY (see CLARENCE)

Margaret GASCOIGNE = Sir Christopher WARDE

Anne WARDE = Ralph NEVILLE

Katherine NEVILLE = Sir Walter STRICKLAND

Walter STRICKLAND = (1) Agnes (HAMERTON?)

(or illegitimate) Ellen STRICKLAND = John CARLETON

Walter CARLETON = Jane GIBBON

Edward CARLETON of Mass. = Ellen NEWTON

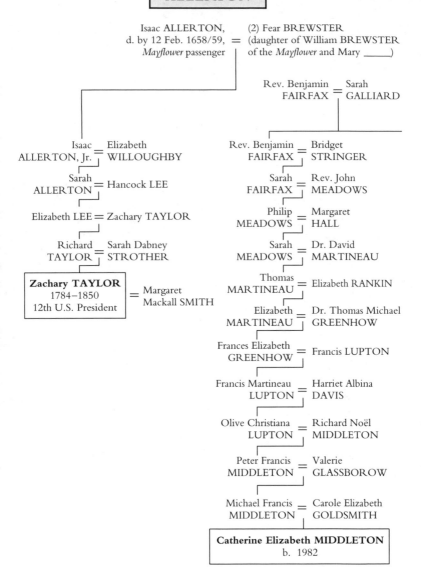

ALLERTON

Isaac ALLERTON, d. by 12 Feb. 1658/59, *Mayflower* passenger = (2) Fear BREWSTER (daughter of William BREWSTER of the *Mayflower* and Mary _____)

Rev. Benjamin FAIRFAX = Sarah GALLIARD

Isaac ALLERTON, Jr. = Elizabeth WILLOUGHBY

Rev. Benjamin FAIRFAX = Bridget STRINGER

Sarah ALLERTON = Hancock LEE

Sarah FAIRFAX = Rev. John MEADOWS

Elizabeth LEE = Zachary TAYLOR

Philip MEADOWS = Margaret HALL

Richard TAYLOR = Sarah Dabney STROTHER

Sarah MEADOWS = Dr. David MARTINEAU

Zachary TAYLOR 1784–1850 12th U.S. President = Margaret Mackall SMITH

Thomas MARTINEAU = Elizabeth RANKIN

Elizabeth MARTINEAU = Dr. Thomas Michael GREENHOW

Frances Elizabeth GREENHOW = Francis LUPTON

Francis Martineau LUPTON = Harriet Albina DAVIS

Olive Christiana LUPTON = Richard Noël MIDDLETON

Peter Francis MIDDLETON = Valerie GLASSBOROW

Michael Francis MIDDLETON = Carole Elizabeth GOLDSMITH

Catherine Elizabeth MIDDLETON b. 1982

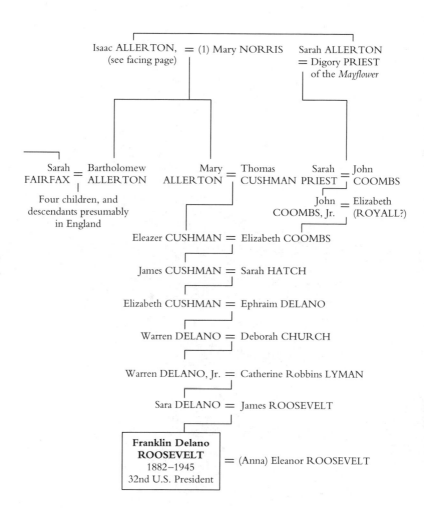

Isaac ALLERTON, = (1) Mary NORRIS
(see facing page)

Sarah ALLERTON
= Digory PRIEST
of the *Mayflower*

Sarah _ Bartholomew
FAIRFAX ⫟ ALLERTON

Four children, and
descendants presumably
in England

Mary _ Thomas
ALLERTON ⫟ CUSHMAN

Sarah _ John
PRIEST ⫟ COOMBS

John _ Elizabeth
COOMBS, Jr. ⫟ (ROYALL?)

Eleazer CUSHMAN = Elizabeth COOMBS

James CUSHMAN = Sarah HATCH

Elizabeth CUSHMAN = Ephraim DELANO

Warren DELANO = Deborah CHURCH

Warren DELANO, Jr. = Catherine Robbins LYMAN

Sara DELANO = James ROOSEVELT

**Franklin Delano
ROOSEVELT**
1882–1945
32nd U.S. President

= (Anna) Eleanor ROOSEVELT

III.
American Cousins
of Catherine Middleton

ELLEN DeGENERES

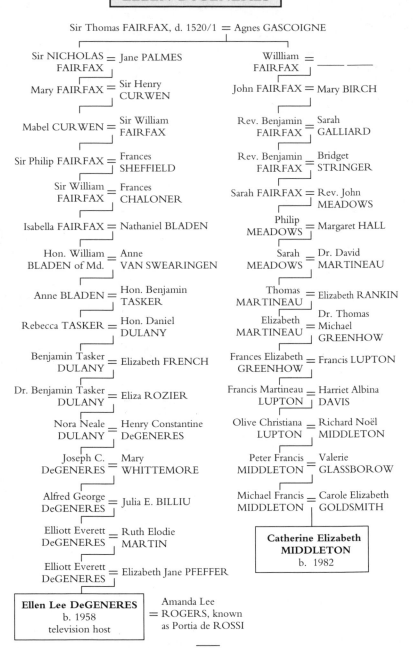

Sir Thomas FAIRFAX, d. 1520/1 = Agnes GASCOIGNE

Sir NICHOLAS FAIRFAX = Jane PALMES

Willliam FAIRFAX = ——— ———

Mary FAIRFAX = Sir Henry CURWEN

John FAIRFAX = Mary BIRCH

Mabel CURWEN = Sir William FAIRFAX

Rev. Benjamin FAIRFAX = Sarah GALLIARD

Sir Philip FAIRFAX = Frances SHEFFIELD

Rev. Benjamin FAIRFAX = Bridget STRINGER

Sir William FAIRFAX = Frances CHALONER

Sarah FAIRFAX = Rev. John MEADOWS

Isabella FAIRFAX = Nathaniel BLADEN

Philip MEADOWS = Margaret HALL

Hon. William BLADEN of Md. = Anne VAN SWEARINGEN

Sarah MEADOWS = Dr. David MARTINEAU

Anne BLADEN = Hon. Benjamin TASKER

Thomas MARTINEAU = Elizabeth RANKIN

Rebecca TASKER = Hon. Daniel DULANY

Elizabeth MARTINEAU = Dr. Thomas Michael GREENHOW

Benjamin Tasker DULANY = Elizabeth FRENCH

Frances Elizabeth GREENHOW = Francis LUPTON

Dr. Benjamin Tasker DULANY = Eliza ROZIER

Francis Martineau LUPTON = Harriet Albina DAVIS

Nora Neale DULANY = Henry Constantine DeGENERES

Olive Christiana LUPTON = Richard Noël MIDDLETON

Joseph C. DeGENERES = Mary WHITTEMORE

Peter Francis MIDDLETON = Valerie GLASSBOROW

Alfred George DeGENERES = Julia E. BILLIU

Michael Francis MIDDLETON = Carole Elizabeth GOLDSMITH

Elliott Everett DeGENERES = Ruth Elodie MARTIN

Elliott Everett DeGENERES = Elizabeth Jane PFEFFER

Catherine Elizabeth MIDDLETON
b. 1982

Ellen Lee DeGENERES
b. 1958
television host

Amanda Lee = ROGERS, known as Portia de ROSSI

GEORGE WASHINGTON

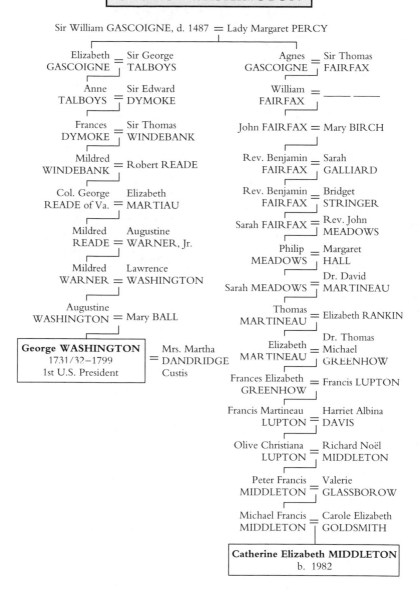

Sir William GASCOIGNE, d. 1487 = Lady Margaret PERCY

Elizabeth = Sir George
GASCOIGNE = TALBOYS

Anne = Sir Edward
TALBOYS = DYMOKE

Frances = Sir Thomas
DYMOKE = WINDEBANK

Mildred = Robert READE
WINDEBANK

Col. George   Elizabeth
READE of Va. = MARTIAU

Mildred   Augustine
READE = WARNER, Jr.

Mildred   Lawrence
WARNER = WASHINGTON

Augustine
WASHINGTON = Mary BALL

George WASHINGTON   Mrs. Martha
1731/32–1799   = DANDRIDGE
1st U.S. President   Custis

Agnes = Sir Thomas
GASCOIGNE = FAIRFAX

William =
FAIRFAX

John FAIRFAX = Mary BIRCH

Rev. Benjamin = Sarah
FAIRFAX = GALLIARD

Rev. Benjamin = Bridget
FAIRFAX = STRINGER

Sarah FAIRFAX = Rev. John
MEADOWS

Philip = Margaret
MEADOWS = HALL

Sarah MEADOWS = Dr. David
MARTINEAU

Thomas
MARTINEAU = Elizabeth RANKIN

Elizabeth = Dr. Thomas
MARTINEAU = Michael
GREENHOW

Frances Elizabeth = Francis LUPTON
GREENHOW

Francis Martineau   Harriet Albina
LUPTON = DAVIS

Olive Christiana   Richard Noël
LUPTON = MIDDLETON

Peter Francis   Valerie
MIDDLETON = GLASSBOROW

Michael Francis   Carole Elizabeth
MIDDLETON = GOLDSMITH

Catherine Elizabeth MIDDLETON
b. 1982

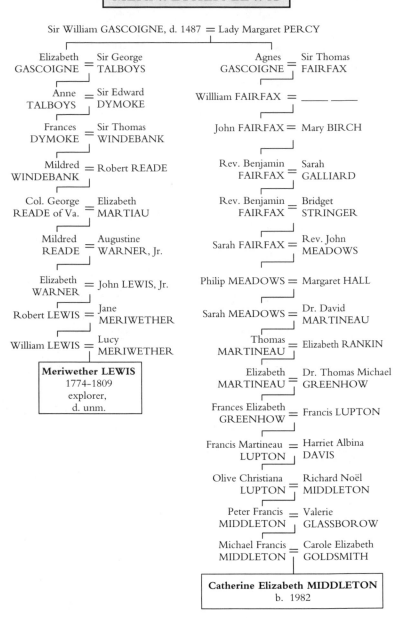

MERIWETHER LEWIS

Sir William GASCOIGNE, d. 1487 = Lady Margaret PERCY

Elizabeth GASCOIGNE = Sir George TALBOYS

Anne TALBOYS = Sir Edward DYMOKE

Frances DYMOKE = Sir Thomas WINDEBANK

Mildred WINDEBANK = Robert READE

Col. George READE of Va. = Elizabeth MARTIAU

Mildred READE = Augustine WARNER, Jr.

Elizabeth WARNER = John LEWIS, Jr.

Robert LEWIS = Jane MERIWETHER

William LEWIS = Lucy MERIWETHER

Meriwether LEWIS
1774–1809
explorer,
d. unm.

Agnes GASCOIGNE = Sir Thomas FAIRFAX

Willliam FAIRFAX = _____ _____

John FAIRFAX = Mary BIRCH

Rev. Benjamin FAIRFAX = Sarah GALLIARD

Rev. Benjamin FAIRFAX = Bridget STRINGER

Sarah FAIRFAX = Rev. John MEADOWS

Philip MEADOWS = Margaret HALL

Sarah MEADOWS = Dr. David MARTINEAU

Thomas MARTINEAU = Elizabeth RANKIN

Elizabeth MARTINEAU = Dr. Thomas Michael GREENHOW

Frances Elizabeth GREENHOW = Francis LUPTON

Francis Martineau LUPTON = Harriet Albina DAVIS

Olive Christiana LUPTON = Richard Noël MIDDLETON

Peter Francis MIDDLETON = Valerie GLASSBOROW

Michael Francis MIDDLETON = Carole Elizabeth GOLDSMITH

Catherine Elizabeth MIDDLETON
b. 1982

GENERAL GEORGE SMITH PATTON, Jr.

Sir William GASCOIGNE, d. 1487 = Lady Margaret PERCY

Elizabeth GASCOIGNE = Sir George TALBOYS

Agnes GASCOIGNE = Sir Thomas FAIRFAX

Anne TALBOYS = Sir Edward DYMOKE

William FAIRFAX = _____ _____

Frances DYMOKE = Sir Thomas WINDEBANK

John FAIRFAX = Mary BIRCH

Mildred WINDEBANK = Robert READE

Rev. Benjamin FAIRFAX = Sarah GALLIARD

Col. George READE of Va. = Elizabeth MARTIAU

Rev. Benjamin FAIRFAX = Bridget STRINGER

Thomas READE = Lucy GWYNE

Sarah FAIRFAX = Rev. John MEADOWS

Mildred READE = Philip ROOTES

Philip MEADOWS = Margaret HALL

Elizabeth ROOTES = Rev. John THOMPSON

Sarah MEADOWS = Dr. David MARTINEAU

Philip Rootes THOMPSON = Anna DAVENPORT

Thomas MARTINEAU = Elizabeth RANKIN

Eleanor THOMPSON = William THORNTON, Jr.

Elizabeth MARTINEAU = Dr. Thomas Michael GREENHOW

Susanna Thompson THORNTON = Andrew GLASSELL, Jr.

Frances Elizabeth GREENHOW = Francis LUPTON

Susan Thornton GLASSELL = George Smith PATTON

Francis Martineau LUPTON = Harriet Albina DAVIS

George Smith PATTON = Ruth Wilson

Olive Christiana LUPTON = Richard Noël MIDDLETON

George Smith PATTON Jr.
1885-1945
Word War II army commander

Peter Francis MIDDLETON = Valerie GLASSBOROW

= Beatrice Banning AYER

Michael Francis MIDDLETON = Carole Elizabeth GOLDSMITH

Catherine Elizabeth MIDDLETON
b. 1982

HENRY BROOKS ADAMS / PHILLIPS BROOKS / LEVERETT SALTONSTALL

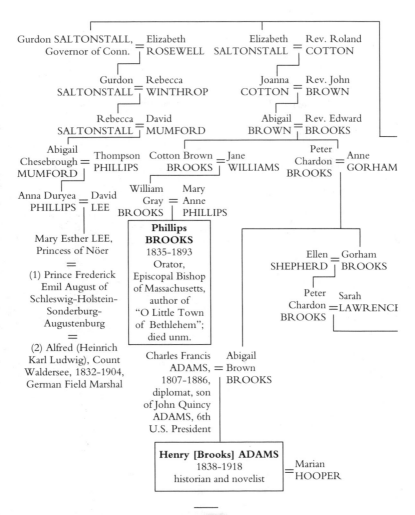

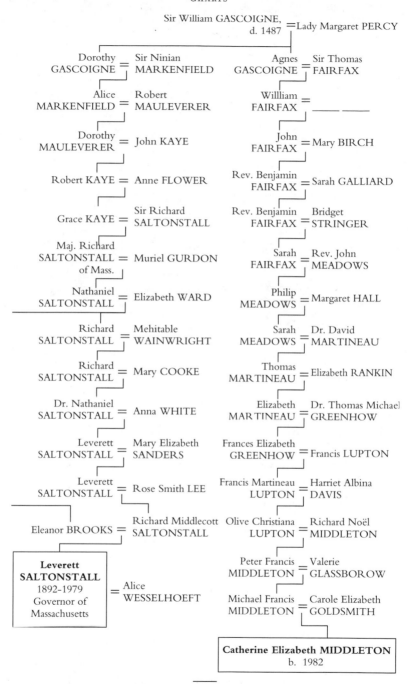

Sir William GASCOIGNE, d. 1487 = Lady Margaret PERCY

Dorothy GASCOIGNE = Sir Ninian MARKENFIELD
Agnes GASCOIGNE = Sir Thomas FAIRFAX

Alice MARKENFIELD = Robert MAULEVERER
Willliam FAIRFAX = _____ _____

Dorothy MAULEVERER = John KAYE
John FAIRFAX = Mary BIRCH

Robert KAYE = Anne FLOWER
Rev. Benjamin FAIRFAX = Sarah GALLIARD

Grace KAYE = Sir Richard SALTONSTALL
Rev. Benjamin FAIRFAX = Bridget STRINGER

Maj. Richard SALTONSTALL of Mass. = Muriel GURDON
Sarah FAIRFAX = Rev. John MEADOWS

Nathaniel SALTONSTALL = Elizabeth WARD
Philip MEADOWS = Margaret HALL

Richard SALTONSTALL = Mehitable WAINWRIGHT
Sarah MEADOWS = Dr. David MARTINEAU

Richard SALTONSTALL = Mary COOKE
Thomas MARTINEAU = Elizabeth RANKIN

Dr. Nathaniel SALTONSTALL = Anna WHITE
Elizabeth MARTINEAU = Dr. Thomas Michael GREENHOW

Leverett SALTONSTALL = Mary Elizabeth SANDERS
Frances Elizabeth GREENHOW = Francis LUPTON

Leverett SALTONSTALL = Rose Smith LEE
Francis Martineau LUPTON = Harriet Albina DAVIS

Eleanor BROOKS = Richard Middlecott SALTONSTALL
Olive Christiana LUPTON = Richard Noël MIDDLETON

Leverett SALTONSTALL 1892-1979 Governor of Massachusetts = Alice WESSELHOEFT
Peter Francis MIDDLETON = Valerie GLASSBOROW

Michael Francis MIDDLETON = Carole Elizabeth GOLDSMITH

Catherine Elizabeth MIDDLETON b. 1982

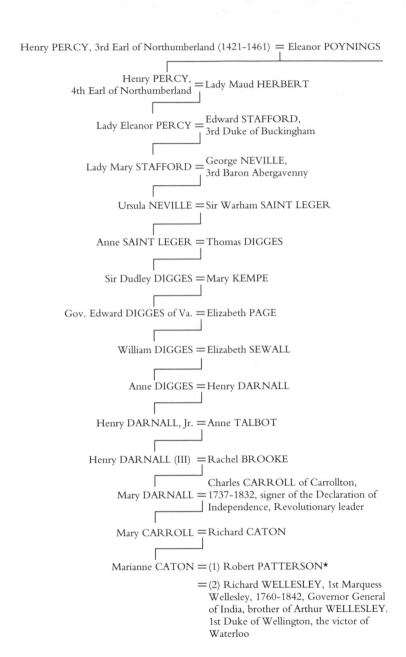

Henry PERCY, 3rd Earl of Northumberland (1421-1461) = Eleanor POYNINGS

Henry PERCY,
4th Earl of Northumberland = Lady Maud HERBERT

Lady Eleanor PERCY = Edward STAFFORD,
3rd Duke of Buckingham

Lady Mary STAFFORD = George NEVILLE,
3rd Baron Abergavenny

Ursula NEVILLE = Sir Warham SAINT LEGER

Anne SAINT LEGER = Thomas DIGGES

Sir Dudley DIGGES = Mary KEMPE

Gov. Edward DIGGES of Va. = Elizabeth PAGE

William DIGGES = Elizabeth SEWALL

Anne DIGGES = Henry DARNALL

Henry DARNALL, Jr. = Anne TALBOT

Henry DARNALL (III) = Rachel BROOKE

Mary DARNALL = Charles CARROLL of Carrollton,
1737-1832, signer of the Declaration of
Independence, Revolutionary leader

Mary CARROLL = Richard CATON

Marianne CATON = (1) Robert PATTERSON★

= (2) Richard WELLESLEY, 1st Marquess
Wellesley, 1760-1842, Governor General
of India, brother of Arthur WELLESLEY,
1st Duke of Wellington, the victor of
Waterloo

★ His sister, Elizabeth PATTERSON, was the first wife of Jerome BONAPARTE, King of Westphalia,
brother of Napoleon I. The 1st Marquess WELLESLEY is an ancestor, by his first wife, of the Queen Mother.

MARIANNE CATON, MARCHIONESS WELLESLEY

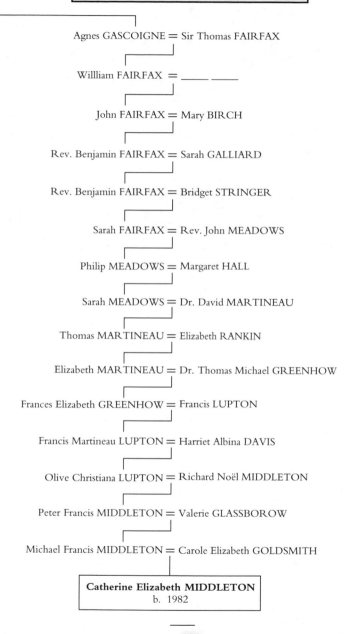

Agnes GASCOIGNE = Sir Thomas FAIRFAX

Willliam FAIRFAX = _____ _____

John FAIRFAX = Mary BIRCH

Rev. Benjamin FAIRFAX = Sarah GALLIARD

Rev. Benjamin FAIRFAX = Bridget STRINGER

Sarah FAIRFAX = Rev. John MEADOWS

Philip MEADOWS = Margaret HALL

Sarah MEADOWS = Dr. David MARTINEAU

Thomas MARTINEAU = Elizabeth RANKIN

Elizabeth MARTINEAU = Dr. Thomas Michael GREENHOW

Frances Elizabeth GREENHOW = Francis LUPTON

Francis Martineau LUPTON = Harriet Albina DAVIS

Olive Christiana LUPTON = Richard Noël MIDDLETON

Peter Francis MIDDLETON = Valerie GLASSBOROW

Michael Francis MIDDLETON = Carole Elizabeth GOLDSMITH

Catherine Elizabeth MIDDLETON
b. 1982

RICHARD EVELYN BYRD

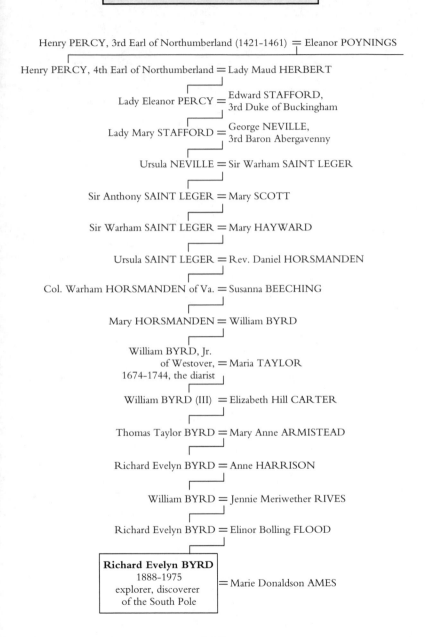

Henry PERCY, 3rd Earl of Northumberland (1421-1461) = Eleanor POYNINGS

Henry PERCY, 4th Earl of Northumberland = Lady Maud HERBERT

Lady Eleanor PERCY = Edward STAFFORD, 3rd Duke of Buckingham

Lady Mary STAFFORD = George NEVILLE, 3rd Baron Abergavenny

Ursula NEVILLE = Sir Warham SAINT LEGER

Sir Anthony SAINT LEGER = Mary SCOTT

Sir Warham SAINT LEGER = Mary HAYWARD

Ursula SAINT LEGER = Rev. Daniel HORSMANDEN

Col. Warham HORSMANDEN of Va. = Susanna BEECHING

Mary HORSMANDEN = William BYRD

William BYRD, Jr. of Westover, 1674-1744, the diarist = Maria TAYLOR

William BYRD (III) = Elizabeth Hill CARTER

Thomas Taylor BYRD = Mary Anne ARMISTEAD

Richard Evelyn BYRD = Anne HARRISON

William BYRD = Jennie Meriwether RIVES

Richard Evelyn BYRD = Elinor Bolling FLOOD

Richard Evelyn BYRD
1888-1975
explorer, discoverer
of the South Pole
= Marie Donaldson AMES

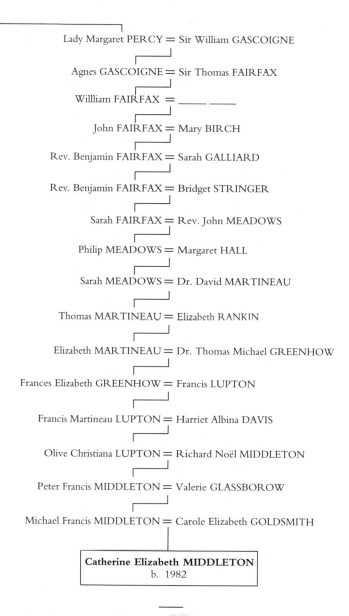

Lady Margaret PERCY = Sir William GASCOIGNE

Agnes GASCOIGNE = Sir Thomas FAIRFAX

Willliam FAIRFAX = _____ _____

John FAIRFAX = Mary BIRCH

Rev. Benjamin FAIRFAX = Sarah GALLIARD

Rev. Benjamin FAIRFAX = Bridget STRINGER

Sarah FAIRFAX = Rev. John MEADOWS

Philip MEADOWS = Margaret HALL

Sarah MEADOWS = Dr. David MARTINEAU

Thomas MARTINEAU = Elizabeth RANKIN

Elizabeth MARTINEAU = Dr. Thomas Michael GREENHOW

Frances Elizabeth GREENHOW = Francis LUPTON

Francis Martineau LUPTON = Harriet Albina DAVIS

Olive Christiana LUPTON = Richard Noël MIDDLETON

Peter Francis MIDDLETON = Valerie GLASSBOROW

Michael Francis MIDDLETON = Carole Elizabeth GOLDSMITH

Catherine Elizabeth MIDDLETON
b. 1982

UPTON BEALL SINCLAIR, Jr.

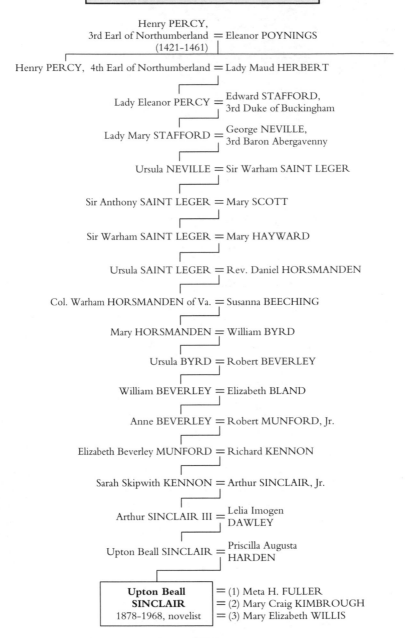

Henry PERCY,
3rd Earl of Northumberland = Eleanor POYNINGS
(1421–1461)

Henry PERCY, 4th Earl of Northumberland = Lady Maud HERBERT

Lady Eleanor PERCY = Edward STAFFORD,
3rd Duke of Buckingham

Lady Mary STAFFORD = George NEVILLE,
3rd Baron Abergavenny

Ursula NEVILLE = Sir Warham SAINT LEGER

Sir Anthony SAINT LEGER = Mary SCOTT

Sir Warham SAINT LEGER = Mary HAYWARD

Ursula SAINT LEGER = Rev. Daniel HORSMANDEN

Col. Warham HORSMANDEN of Va. = Susanna BEECHING

Mary HORSMANDEN = William BYRD

Ursula BYRD = Robert BEVERLEY

William BEVERLEY = Elizabeth BLAND

Anne BEVERLEY = Robert MUNFORD, Jr.

Elizabeth Beverley MUNFORD = Richard KENNON

Sarah Skipwith KENNON = Arthur SINCLAIR, Jr.

Arthur SINCLAIR III = Lelia Imogen
DAWLEY

Upton Beall SINCLAIR = Priscilla Augusta
HARDEN

**Upton Beall
SINCLAIR**
1878-1968, novelist
= (1) Meta H. FULLER
= (2) Mary Craig KIMBROUGH
= (3) Mary Elizabeth WILLIS

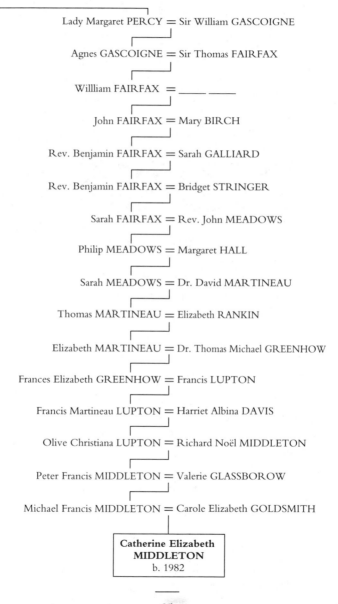

Lady Margaret PERCY = Sir William GASCOIGNE

Agnes GASCOIGNE = Sir Thomas FAIRFAX

Willliam FAIRFAX = _____ _____

John FAIRFAX = Mary BIRCH

Rev. Benjamin FAIRFAX = Sarah GALLIARD

Rev. Benjamin FAIRFAX = Bridget STRINGER

Sarah FAIRFAX = Rev. John MEADOWS

Philip MEADOWS = Margaret HALL

Sarah MEADOWS = Dr. David MARTINEAU

Thomas MARTINEAU = Elizabeth RANKIN

Elizabeth MARTINEAU = Dr. Thomas Michael GREENHOW

Frances Elizabeth GREENHOW = Francis LUPTON

Francis Martineau LUPTON = Harriet Albina DAVIS

Olive Christiana LUPTON = Richard Noël MIDDLETON

Peter Francis MIDDLETON = Valerie GLASSBOROW

Michael Francis MIDDLETON = Carole Elizabeth GOLDSMITH

**Catherine Elizabeth
MIDDLETON**
b. 1982

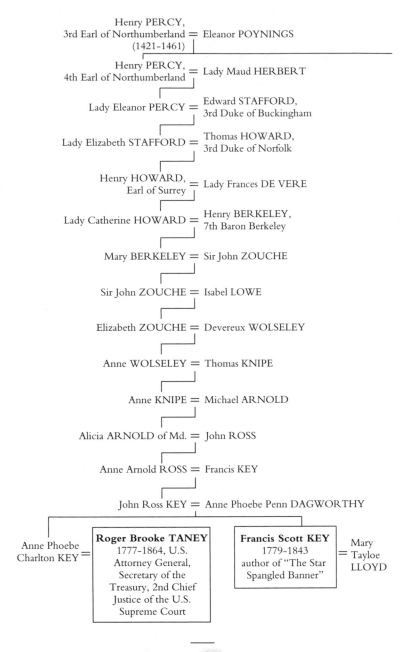

Henry PERCY,
3rd Earl of Northumberland = Eleanor POYNINGS
(1421–1461)

Henry PERCY, = Lady Maud HERBERT
4th Earl of Northumberland

Lady Eleanor PERCY = Edward STAFFORD,
3rd Duke of Buckingham

Lady Elizabeth STAFFORD = Thomas HOWARD,
3rd Duke of Norfolk

Henry HOWARD, = Lady Frances DE VERE
Earl of Surrey

Lady Catherine HOWARD = Henry BERKELEY,
7th Baron Berkeley

Mary BERKELEY = Sir John ZOUCHE

Sir John ZOUCHE = Isabel LOWE

Elizabeth ZOUCHE = Devereux WOLSELEY

Anne WOLSELEY = Thomas KNIPE

Anne KNIPE = Michael ARNOLD

Alicia ARNOLD of Md. = John ROSS

Anne Arnold ROSS = Francis KEY

John Ross KEY = Anne Phoebe Penn DAGWORTHY

Anne Phoebe
Charlton KEY =
Roger Brooke TANEY
1777–1864, U.S.
Attorney General,
Secretary of the
Treasury, 2nd Chief
Justice of the U.S.
Supreme Court

Francis Scott KEY
1779–1843
author of "The Star
Spangled Banner" =
Mary
Tayloe
LLOYD

FRANCIS SCOTT KEY and
Mrs. ROGER BROOKE TANEY

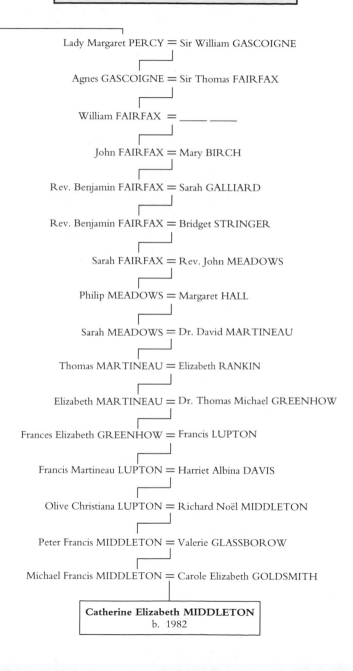

Lady Margaret PERCY = Sir William GASCOIGNE

Agnes GASCOIGNE = Sir Thomas FAIRFAX

William FAIRFAX = _____ _____

John FAIRFAX = Mary BIRCH

Rev. Benjamin FAIRFAX = Sarah GALLIARD

Rev. Benjamin FAIRFAX = Bridget STRINGER

Sarah FAIRFAX = Rev. John MEADOWS

Philip MEADOWS = Margaret HALL

Sarah MEADOWS = Dr. David MARTINEAU

Thomas MARTINEAU = Elizabeth RANKIN

Elizabeth MARTINEAU = Dr. Thomas Michael GREENHOW

Frances Elizabeth GREENHOW = Francis LUPTON

Francis Martineau LUPTON = Harriet Albina DAVIS

Olive Christiana LUPTON = Richard Noël MIDDLETON

Peter Francis MIDDLETON = Valerie GLASSBOROW

Michael Francis MIDDLETON = Carole Elizabeth GOLDSMITH

Catherine Elizabeth MIDDLETON
b. 1982

IV.
British and European
Cousins of Catherine Middleton

GUY STUART RITCHIE

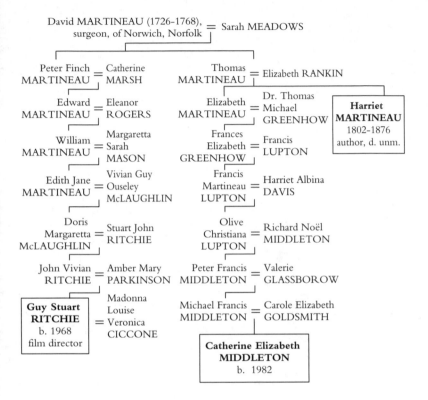

David MARTINEAU (1726-1768), = Sarah MEADOWS
surgeon, of Norwich, Norfolk

Peter Finch = Catherine
MARTINEAU MARSH

Thomas = Elizabeth RANKIN
MARTINEAU

Edward = Eleanor
MARTINEAU ROGERS

Elizabeth = Dr. Thomas
MARTINEAU Michael
GREENHOW

Harriet MARTINEAU
1802-1876
author, d. unm.

William = Margaretta
MARTINEAU Sarah
MASON

Frances = Francis
Elizabeth LUPTON
GREENHOW

Edith Jane = Vivian Guy
MARTINEAU Ouseley
McLAUGHLIN

Francis = Harriet Albina
Martineau DAVIS
LUPTON

Doris = Stuart John
Margaretta RITCHIE
McLAUGHLIN

Olive = Richard Noël
Christiana MIDDLETON
LUPTON

John Vivian = Amber Mary
RITCHIE PARKINSON

Peter Francis = Valerie
MIDDLETON GLASSBOROW

Guy Stuart RITCHIE
b. 1968
film director
= Madonna
Louise
Veronica
CICCONE

Michael Francis = Carole Elizabeth
MIDDLETON GOLDSMITH

Catherine Elizabeth MIDDLETON
b. 1982

ARTHUR JAMES BALFOUR, 1st EARL of BALFOUR, and LADY RAYLEIGH

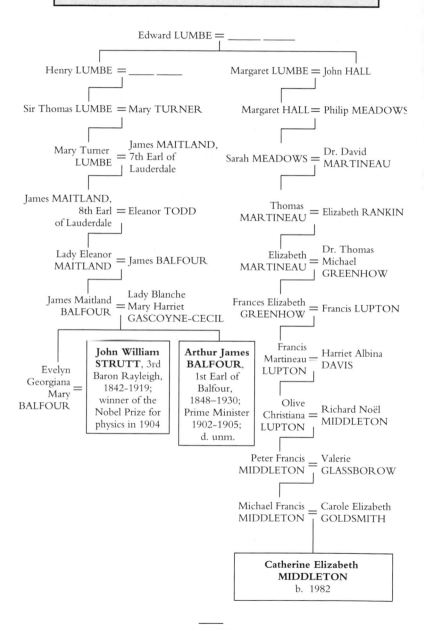

ARTHUR CHARLES VALERIAN WELLESLEY, MARQUESS OF DOURO

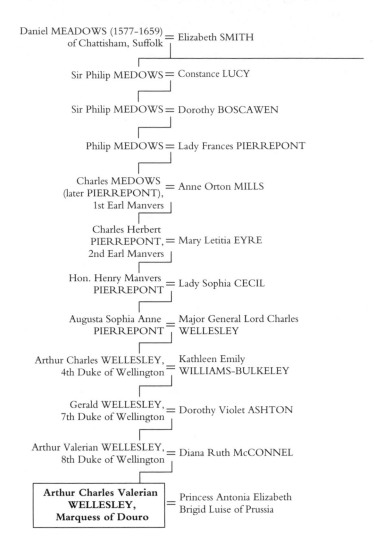

Daniel MEADOWS (1577-1659) of Chattisham, Suffolk = Elizabeth SMITH

Sir Philip MEDOWS = Constance LUCY

Sir Philip MEDOWS = Dorothy BOSCAWEN

Philip MEDOWS = Lady Frances PIERREPONT

Charles MEDOWS (later PIERREPONT), 1st Earl Manvers = Anne Orton MILLS

Charles Herbert PIERREPONT, 2nd Earl Manvers = Mary Letitia EYRE

Hon. Henry Manvers PIERREPONT = Lady Sophia CECIL

Augusta Sophia Anne PIERREPONT = Major General Lord Charles WELLESLEY

Arthur Charles WELLESLEY, 4th Duke of Wellington = Kathleen Emily WILLIAMS-BULKELEY

Gerald WELLESLEY, 7th Duke of Wellington = Dorothy Violet ASHTON

Arthur Valerian WELLESLEY, 8th Duke of Wellington = Diana Ruth McCONNEL

Arthur Charles Valerian WELLESLEY, Marquess of Douro = Princess Antonia Elizabeth Brigid Luise of Prussia

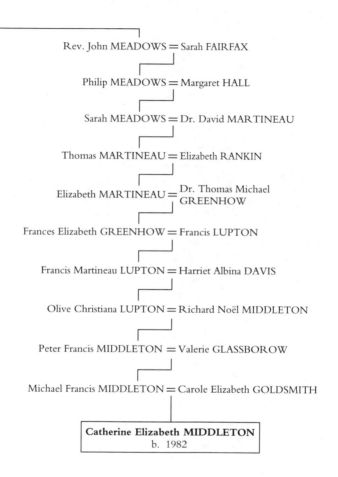

Rev. John MEADOWS = Sarah FAIRFAX

Philip MEADOWS = Margaret HALL

Sarah MEADOWS = Dr. David MARTINEAU

Thomas MARTINEAU = Elizabeth RANKIN

Elizabeth MARTINEAU = Dr. Thomas Michael GREENHOW

Frances Elizabeth GREENHOW = Francis LUPTON

Francis Martineau LUPTON = Harriet Albina DAVIS

Olive Christiana LUPTON = Richard Noël MIDDLETON

Peter Francis MIDDLETON = Valerie GLASSBOROW

Michael Francis MIDDLETON = Carole Elizabeth GOLDSMITH

Catherine Elizabeth MIDDLETON
b. 1982

Henry PERCY,
3rd Earl of Northumberland (1421–1461) = Eleanor POYNINGS

Henry PERCY, 4th Earl of Northumberland = Lady Maud HERBERT

Lady Eleanor PERCY = Edward STAFFORD,
3rd Duke of Buckingham

Lady Mary STAFFORD = George NEVILLE, 3rd Baron
Abergavenny

Ursula NEVILLE = Sir Warham SAINT LEGER

Sir Anthony SAINT LEGER = Mary SCOTT

Sir Warham SAINT LEGER = Mary HAYWARD

Ursula SAINT LEGER = Rev. Daniel HORSMANDEN

Col. Warham HORSMANDEN of Va. = Susanna BEECHING

Mary HORSMANDEN = William BYRD

William BYRD, Jr. of Westover,
1674–1744, the diarist = Maria TAYLOR

Maria BYRD = Landon CARTER

Maria CARTER = Robert BEVERLEY

Anna Mumford BEVERLEY = Francis CORBIN

Francis Porteus CORBIN = Agnes Rebecca HAMILTON

Elizabeth Tayloe CORBIN = Louis Pol Henri,
Vicomte de DAMPIERRE

Louis Frétard Charles
Henri Richard de DAMPIERRE, = Jeanne Maria Charlotte
1st Duke of San Lorenzo Nuovo CARRABY

Roger Richard Charles
Henri Etienne de DAMPIERRE, = Vittoria Emilia Ipsycrathea
2nd Duke of San Lorenzo Nuovo Agricola RUSPOLI

Victoria Jeanne Joséphine Pierre = HRH Infante Don Jaime Luitpold
Marie Emanuela de DAMPIERRE Isabelito Enrique Alejandro Alberto
Victor Acacio Pedro Pablo María of
Spain, 1st Duke of Segovia, 1908–1975

Don Alfonso Jaime Marcelino María del Carmen Esperanza Alejandra
Manuel Victor María de de la Santissima Trinidad y de Todos los
BORBON y de DAMPIERRE, = Santos MARTÍNEZ-BORDIÚ Y
1st Duke of Cádiz, 1936–1989, the FRANCO, granddaughter of Francisco
legitimist heir of Spain and France FRANCO, longtime dictator of Spain

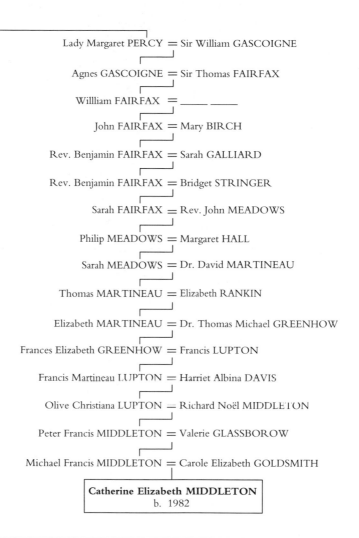

Lady Margaret PERCY = Sir William GASCOIGNE

Agnes GASCOIGNE = Sir Thomas FAIRFAX

Willliam FAIRFAX = ____ ____

John FAIRFAX = Mary BIRCH

Rev. Benjamin FAIRFAX = Sarah GALLIARD

Rev. Benjamin FAIRFAX = Bridget STRINGER

Sarah FAIRFAX = Rev. John MEADOWS

Philip MEADOWS = Margaret HALL

Sarah MEADOWS = Dr. David MARTINEAU

Thomas MARTINEAU = Elizabeth RANKIN

Elizabeth MARTINEAU = Dr. Thomas Michael GREENHOW

Frances Elizabeth GREENHOW = Francis LUPTON

Francis Martineau LUPTON = Harriet Albina DAVIS

Olive Christiana LUPTON = Richard Noël MIDDLETON

Peter Francis MIDDLETON = Valerie GLASSBOROW

Michael Francis MIDDLETON = Carole Elizabeth GOLDSMITH

Catherine Elizabeth MIDDLETON
b. 1982

**DON ALFONSO de BORBON y de DAMPIERRE,
1st DUKE of CÁDIZ**

V.
The English
Royal Family since 1603

CharTS
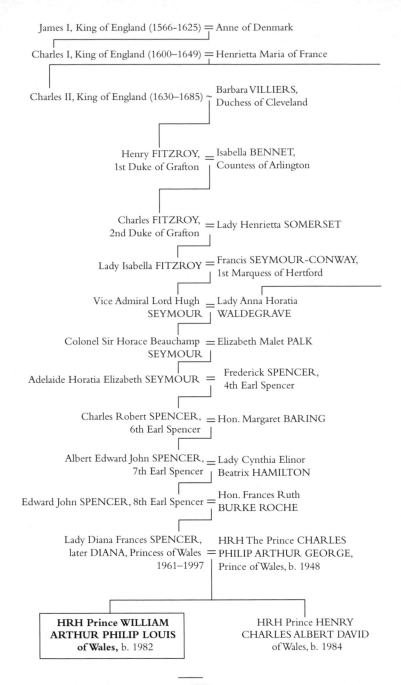

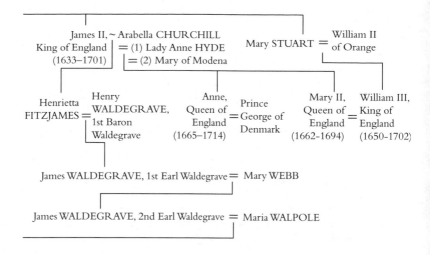

James II, ~ Arabella CHURCHILL
King of England = (1) Lady Anne HYDE
(1633–1701) = (2) Mary of Modena

Mary STUART = William II of Orange

Henrietta FITZJAMES = Henry WALDEGRAVE, 1st Baron Waldegrave

Anne, Queen of England (1665–1714) = Prince George of Denmark

Mary II, Queen of England (1662-1694) = William III, King of England (1650-1702)

James WALDEGRAVE, 1st Earl Waldegrave = Mary WEBB

James WALDEGRAVE, 2nd Earl Waldegrave = Maria WALPOLE

**From JAMES I to
DIANA, PRINCESS of WALES**

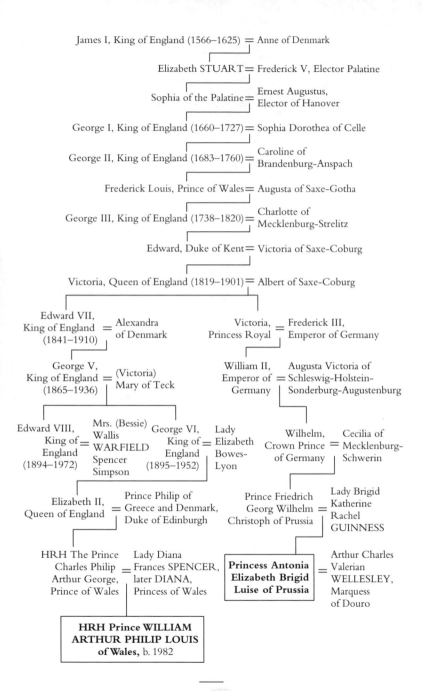

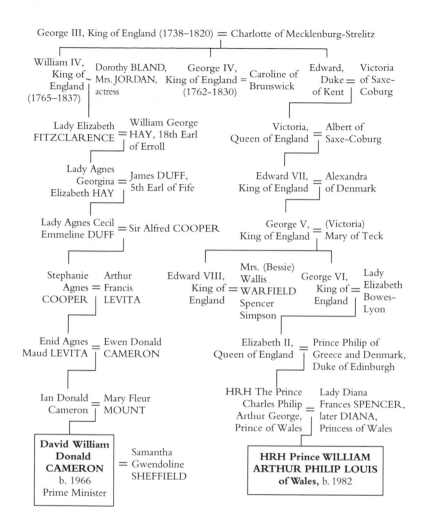

George III, King of England (1738–1820) = Charlotte of Mecklenburg-Strelitz

William IV, King of England (1765–1837) ~ Dorothy BLAND, Mrs. JORDAN, actress

George IV, King of England (1762-1830) = Caroline of Brunswick

Edward, Duke of Kent = Victoria of Saxe-Coburg

Lady Elizabeth FITZCLARENCE = William George HAY, 18th Earl of Erroll

Victoria, Queen of England = Albert of Saxe-Coburg

Lady Agnes Georgina Elizabeth HAY = James DUFF, 5th Earl of Fife

Edward VII, King of England = Alexandra of Denmark

Lady Agnes Cecil Emmeline DUFF = Sir Alfred COOPER

George V, King of England = (Victoria) Mary of Teck

Stephanie Agnes COOPER = Arthur Francis LEVITA

Edward VIII, King of England = Mrs. (Bessie) Wallis WARFIELD Spencer Simpson

George VI, King of England = Lady Elizabeth Bowes-Lyon

Enid Agnes Maud LEVITA = Ewen Donald CAMERON

Elizabeth II, Queen of England = Prince Philip of Greece and Denmark, Duke of Edinburgh

Ian Donald Cameron = Mary Fleur MOUNT

HRH The Prince Charles Philip Arthur George, Prince of Wales = Lady Diana Frances SPENCER, later DIANA, Princess of Wales

David William Donald CAMERON b. 1966 Prime Minister = Samantha Gwendoline SHEFFIELD

HRH Prince WILLIAM ARTHUR PHILIP LOUIS of Wales, b. 1982

From JAMES I to PRINCE WILLIAM of WALES, DAVID CAMERON, and ANTONIA, MARCHIONESS OF DOURO

VI.
Distant Relationships
of the Current Royal Family

JOHN of Gaunt,
Duke of Lancaster = (1) Blanche of LANCASTER = (2) Constance of CASTILE
(1340-1399)

HENRY IV, King of England = Lady Mary DE BOHUN

Humphrey, Duke of Gloucester ~ ———— ————

Antigone of Gloucester = Henry GREY, 2nd Earl of Tankerville

Lady Elizabeth GREY = Sir Roger KYNASTON

Emma KYNASTON = John EYTON

Elizabeth EYTON = John TREVOR

Edward TREVOR = Jane LLOYD

John TREVOR = Margaret of Myvyrian

Sir Edward TREVOR = Anne BALLE

Sir John TREVOR = Margaret JEFFREYS

Sir John TREVOR = Jane MOSTYN

Anne TREVOR = Michael HILL

Arthur HILL-TREVOR,
1st Viscount Dungannon = Anne STAFFORD

Hon. Anne HILL-TREVOR = Garret WESLEY,
1st Earl of Mornington

Richard WELLESLEY,
1st Marquesss Wellesley [~/=] Hyacinthe Gabrielle ROLAND

Anne WELLESLEY = Lord William Charles Augustus
CAVENDISH-BENTINCK (*see right*)

Rev. Charles William Frederick
CAVENDISH-BENTINCK = Caroline Louisa BURNABY

Dame Cecilia Nina
CAVENDISH-BENTINCK = Claude George BOWES-LYON,
14th Earl of Strathmore and Kinghorne

See p. 118

= (3) Catherine ROËT

John BEAUFORT, = Lady Margaret HOLAND
1st Marquess of Somerset and Dorset

John BEAUFORT, = Margaret BEAUCHAMP
1st Duke of Somerset

Lady Margaret BEAUFORT = Edmund TUDOR, 1st Earl of Richmond

HENRY VII, King of England = Elizabeth of YORK

HENRY VIII, King of England ~ Mary BOLEYN, sister of Anne BOLEYN, and wife of Sir William CARY★

Catherine CARY = Sir Francis KNOLLYS

Lettice KNOLLYS = Walter DEVEREUX, 1st Earl of Essex

Robert DEVEREUX, = Frances WALSINGHAM
2nd Earl of Essex

Lady Frances DEVEREUX = William SEYMOUR, 2nd Duke of Somerset

Lady Jane SEYMOUR = Charles BOYLE, 3rd Viscount Dungarvan

Charles BOYLE,
2nd Earl of Burlington, = Juliana NOEL
3rd Earl of Cork

Richard BOYLE,
3rd Earl of Burlington, = Lady Dorothy SAVILE
4th Earl of Cork

Charlotte BOYLE, = William CAVENDISH,
Baroness Clifford   4th Duke of Devonshire

Lady Dorothy CAVENDISH = William Henry CAVENDISH-BENTINCK,
3rd Duke of Portland

Anne WELLESLEY = Lord William Charles Augustus
(*see left*)   CAVENDISH-BENTINCK

★ The theory that the children of Mary Bolyen were fathered by Henry VIII, rather than Sir William Cary, is presented by Anthony Hoskins in *Genealogists' Magazine*, 25:9 (March 1997): 345-52. Diana, Princess of Wales, is also a descendant (at least four times over) of Mary Boleyn's son Henry Cary, 1st Baron Hunsdon, also a possible natural son of Henry VIII; see Richard K. Evans, *The Ancestry of Diana, Princess of Wales*, 231, 281, 289, 319.

Sir Thomas FAIRFAX, d. 1520/21 = Agnes GASCOIGNE

Sir NICHOLAS FAIRFAX = Jane PALMES

Margaret FAIRFAX = Sir William BELASYSE

Sir Henry BELASYSE, 1st Baronet = Ursula FAIRFAX

Thomas BELASYSE, = Barbara CHOLMONDELEY
1st Viscount Fauconberg

John BELASYSE, 1st Baron Belasyse = Lady Anne PAULET

Hon. Barbara BELASYSE = Sir John WEBB, 3rd Baronet

Mary WEBB = James WALDEGRAVE,
1st Earl Waldegrave

James WALDEGRAVE, = Maria WALPOLE
2nd Earl Waldegrave

Lady Anna Horatia WALDEGRAVE = Vice Admiral Lord Hugh SEYMOUR

Sir Horace Beauchamp SEYMOUR = Elizabeth Malet PALK

Adelaide Horatia Elizabeth SEYMOUR = Frederick SPENCER, 4th Earl Spencer

Charles Robert SPENCER, = Hon. Margaret BARING
6th Earl Spencer

Albert Edward John SPENCER, = Lady Cynthia Elinor Beatrix HAMILTON
7th Earl Spencer

Edward John SPENCER, = Hon. Frances Ruth BURKE ROCHE
8th Earl Spencer

Lady Diana Frances SPENCER,   HRH The Prince Charles
later DIANA, Princess of Wales = Philip Arthur George,
1961–1997   Prince of Wales, b. 1948

**HRH Prince WILLIAM
ARTHUR PHILIP LOUIS
of Wales,** b. 1982

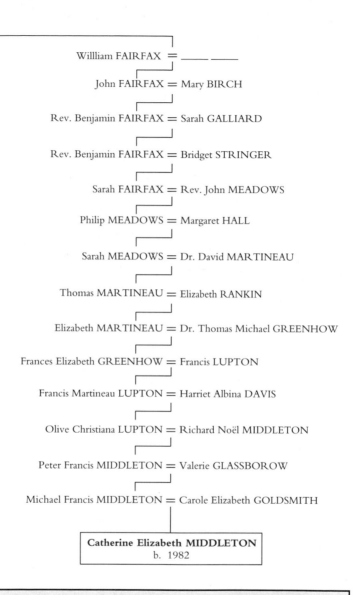

Willliam FAIRFAX = _____ _____

John FAIRFAX = Mary BIRCH

Rev. Benjamin FAIRFAX = Sarah GALLIARD

Rev. Benjamin FAIRFAX = Bridget STRINGER

Sarah FAIRFAX = Rev. John MEADOWS

Philip MEADOWS = Margaret HALL

Sarah MEADOWS = Dr. David MARTINEAU

Thomas MARTINEAU = Elizabeth RANKIN

Elizabeth MARTINEAU = Dr. Thomas Michael GREENHOW

Frances Elizabeth GREENHOW = Francis LUPTON

Francis Martineau LUPTON = Harriet Albina DAVIS

Olive Christiana LUPTON = Richard Noël MIDDLETON

Peter Francis MIDDLETON = Valerie GLASSBOROW

Michael Francis MIDDLETON = Carole Elizabeth GOLDSMITH

Catherine Elizabeth MIDDLETON
b. 1982

The closest relationship between CATHERINE MIDDLETON and PRINCE WILLIAM of WALES via DIANA, PRINCESS of WALES

Sir William GASCOIGNE, d. 1487 = Lady Margaret PERCY

Elizabeth GASCOIGNE = Sir George TALBOYS

Anne TALBOYS = Sir Edward DYMOKE

Frances DYMOKE = Sir Thomas WINDEBANK

Mildred WINDEBANK = Robert READE

Col. George READE of Va. = Elizabeth MARTIAU

Mildred READE = Augustine WARNER, Jr.

Mary WARNER = John SMITH, Jr.

Mildred SMITH = Robert PORTEUS

Robert PORTEUS, Jr. = Judith COCKAYNE

Mildred PORTEUS = Robert HODGSON

Robert HODGSON,
Dean of Carlisle = Mary TUCKER

Henrietta Mildred
HODGSON = Oswald SMITH

Frances Dora SMITH = Claude BOWES-LYON,
13th Earl of Strathmore
and Kinghorne

Claude George BOWES-LYON,
14th Earl of Strathmore = Dame Cecilia Nina
CAVENDISH-
and Kinghorne BENTINCK

HM King GEORGE VI,
King of Great Britain = Lady Elizabeth Angela
Marguerite BOWES-LYON,
1895–1952 HM Queen ELIZABETH
The Queen Mother, 1900–2002

HRH The Prince PHILIP of Greece = HM Queen ELIZABETH II,
and Denmark, Duke of Edinburgh, b. 1921 Queen of Great Britain, b. 1926

Lady Diana Frances SPENCER,
later DIANA, Princess of Wales = HRH The Prince CHARLES
PHILIP ARTHUR GEORGE,
1961–1997 Prince of Wales, b. 1948

**HRH Prince WILLIAM
ARTHUR PHILIP LOUIS of Wales,** b. 1982

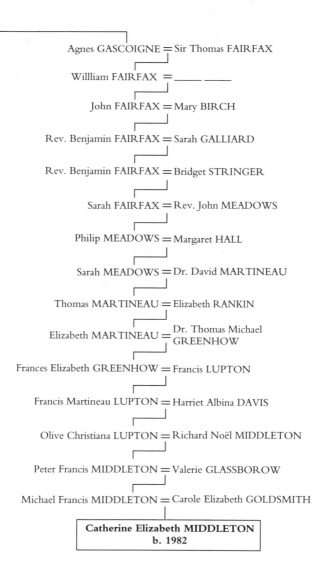

Agnes GASCOIGNE = Sir Thomas FAIRFAX

Willliam FAIRFAX = _____ _____

John FAIRFAX = Mary BIRCH

Rev. Benjamin FAIRFAX = Sarah GALLIARD

Rev. Benjamin FAIRFAX = Bridget STRINGER

Sarah FAIRFAX = Rev. John MEADOWS

Philip MEADOWS = Margaret HALL

Sarah MEADOWS = Dr. David MARTINEAU

Thomas MARTINEAU = Elizabeth RANKIN

Elizabeth MARTINEAU = Dr. Thomas Michael GREENHOW

Frances Elizabeth GREENHOW = Francis LUPTON

Francis Martineau LUPTON = Harriet Albina DAVIS

Olive Christiana LUPTON = Richard Noël MIDDLETON

Peter Francis MIDDLETON = Valerie GLASSBOROW

Michael Francis MIDDLETON = Carole Elizabeth GOLDSMITH

Catherine Elizabeth MIDDLETON
b. 1982

The closest relationship between CATHERINE MIDDLETON and PRINCE WILLIAM of WALES via THE PRINCE of WALES

NOTES

1. Reading/Wokingham district (Berkshire, Buckinghamshire) civil registration indices, 1982, 19: 762, no. 190 (birth), and Claudia Joseph, *Kate: Kate Middleton, Princess in Waiting* (New York, 2009), 118 (birth and baptism); *The Daily Mail*, 17 Nov. 2010, online edition accessed 31 Jan. 2011 (engagement); *The Guardian*, 23 Nov. 2010, online edition accessed 31 Jan. 2011 (wedding place and date).

2. Leeds district (Yorkshire, Northumberland/Westmorland), 1949, 2c: 189, no. 382 (birth); Chiltern and Beaconsfield district (Buckinghamshire), 1980, 19: 1075, no. 473, and Joseph, 117 (marriage); C. A. Lupton, *The Lupton Family in Leeds* (Leeds, 1965), pedigree.

3. Ealing district (Middlesex), 1955, 5e: 68, no. 82 (birth).

4. Joseph, 118, 120.

5. Leeds district (Yorkshire), 1920, 9b: 827, no. 316, and Joseph, 85 (birth); Lupton, pedigree; *The Telegraph*, 17 Nov. 2010, online edition accessed 31 Jan. 2011 (death); Leeds district (Yorkshire—West Riding), 1946, 2c: 316, no. 134 (marriage).

6. Birth registered with the British Consul General at Marseille, France, 1924, entry no. 203 (birth); Joseph, 209 (death).

7. Uxbridge district (Hertfordshire, Oxfordshire, Buckinghamshire, Middlesex), 1931, 3a: 136, no. 133 (birth); West Berkshire district (Berkshire), 2003, 57E: 319/1, no. 85 (death), Ealing district (Middlesex), 1953, 53: 307, no. 428 (marriage).

8. Sunderland district (Durham), 1935, 10: 927, no. 258 (birth); *The Sun,* 5 Aug. 2006, 22 (death).

9. Leeds district (Yorkshire—West Riding), 1879, 9b: 593, no. 433, F. M. Lupton, *Descendants of Charles Hobbs* (Leeds, 1914), 165, and Joseph, 85 (birth); will of Richard Noël Middleton, proved at London 23 Oct. 1951 (death); Leeds district (Yorkshire—West Riding), 1914, 9b: 592, no. 148 (marriage).

10. Joseph, 74 (birth); will of Olive Christiana Middleton, proved at London 3 Feb. 1937 (death); Hobbs, 165; Lupton, 94, 96–97, and pedigree.

11. West Ham district (Essex, Greater London), 1890, 4a: 235, no. 66 (birth); will of Frederick George Glassborow, proved at London 16 Sept. 1954 (death); Marylebone district (Middlesex), 1920, 1a: 1552, no. 211, and Joseph, 103 (marriage).

12. West Ham district (Essex, Greater London), 1888, 4a: 253, no. 18 (birth); will of Constance Glassborow, proved at Oxford 21 Oct. 1977 (death).

13. Brentford district (Middlesex), 1886, 3a: 137, no. 166 (birth); Uxbridge district (Middlesex), 1938, 3a: 126, no. 16 (death, of asthma and acute bronchitis), and Joseph, 47; Uxbridge district (Middlesex), 1909, 3a: 66, no. 38 (marriage).

14. Eton district (Buckinghamshire), 1889, 3a: 641, no. 220 (birth); Hillingdon district (Greater London), 1971, 5c: 897, no. 72.

15. Houghton le Spring district (Durham), 1904, 10: 534, no. 469 (birth); Ealing district (Middlesex), 1976, 12: 196, no. 261 (death, of carcinoma of pancreas), and Joseph, 58; Durham district (Durham), 1934, 10a: 848, no. 42, and Joseph, 29 (marriage).

16. Durham district (Durham), 1903, 10a: 473, no. 147 (birth); Ealing district (London, Middlesex), 1991, 12: 67, and Joseph, 127 (death, of bronchopneumonia, aged 88).

17. Leeds district (Yorkshire—West Riding), 1839, 23: 404, no. 26 (birth); Leeds district (Yorkshire—West Riding), 1887, 9b: 370, no. 456 (death, of angina pectoris); will probated at Wakefield 16 July 1887, *The Times*, London, 19 July 1887, 1a; Frederic Boase, *Modern English Biography*…, 6 vols. (Truro, 1892–1921; reprinted in 1965), 2: 867; Leeds district, 1863, 9b: 476, no. 304 (marriage).

18. Leeds district (Yorkshire—West Riding), 1840, 22: 65, no. 65 (birth); Scarborough district (Yorkshire—East Riding, North Riding), 1889, 9d: 254, no. 169, and Joseph, 68 (death, of typhoid fever).

19. Hunslet district (Yorkshire—West Riding), 1848, 23: 272, no. 56, and Hobbs, 165 (birth); will of Francis Martineau Lupton, proved at Wakefield 10 July 1921 (death); Lupton, 92–97; Leeds district (Yorkshire—West Riding), 1880, 9b: 547, no. 134, and Joseph, 74 (marriage).

20. Hunslet district (Yorkshire—West Riding), 1850, 23: 200, no. 354, Hobbs, 165, and Joseph, 74 (birth); Leeds district (Yorkshire—West Riding), 1892, 9b: 394, no. 235 (death).

21. Shoreditch district (London, Middlesex), 1859, 1c: 201, no. 459 (birth); London Metropolitan Archives, Saint Peter, Hackney, Register of Baptisms, P79/PET (baptism); will of Frederick John Glassborow, proved at London 13 Jan. 1933 (death); West Ham district (Essex, Greater London), 1886, 4a: 89, no. 306 (marriage).

22. Mile End Old Town district (London, Middlesex), 1859, 1c: 301, no. 306 (birth); Bridge district (Kent), 1949, 5b: 73, no. 486 (death, of cerebral thrombosis and cardiac failure).

23. Stepney district (London, Middlesex), 1845, 2: 512, no. 141 (birth); London Metropolitan Archives, Saint James The Great, Hackney, Register of Baptisms, P79/JSG (baptism, where his father is called James); will of Gavin Fullarton Robison, proved at London 24 April 1925 (death); Holbeach district (Lincolnshire), 1875, 7a: 847, no. 343 (marriage).

24. Holbeach district (Lincolnshire), 1852, 7a: 315, no. 391 (birth); Rochford district (Essex), 1922, 4a: 484, no. 424 (death, of cerebral haemorrhage and heart failure; no post mortem).

25. Islington district (Greater London, Middlesex), 1851, 3: 267, no. 15 (birth); Paddington district (Greater London, Middlesex), 1882, 1a: 259, no. 131 (marriage). Joseph, 41, lists the death of a John Goldsmith who died "of exhaustion, melancholia and vascular disease at the age of 68, shortly after the war ended"; this corresponds to the John Goldsmith who died at Long Grove Asylum in Epsom, Surrey 23 Sept. 1919, and whose widow was Jane Matilda Goldsmith. A clerk residing at 39 Bellamy Street in Balham, Surrey, this John Goldsmith left an estate of £754 12s 6d, which would seem unlikely for an elderly bricklayer (Epsom district [Surrey], 1919, 2a: 57, no. 220; *England & Wales, National Probate Calendar [Index of Wills and Administrations], 1861-1941* [online database]).

26. Kensington district (Greater London, Middlesex), 1861, 1a: 122, no. 308 (birth). The death of Jane Goldsmith, 68, was registered in the Brentford district of Middlesex in Jan.-March 1930.

27. Patron submission and Pedigree Resource File of Judith Di-Sandolo of Glamorgan, Wales (birth); Uxbridge district (Middlesex), 1935, 3a: 118, no. 206 (death, of cardiac failure/arteriosclerosis); Eton district (Buckinghamshire), 1868, 3a: 591, no. 218 (marriage).

28. Eton district (Buckinghamshire), 1846, 6: 399, no. 36 (birth); Uxbridge district (Middlesex), 1927, 3a: 58, no. 415 (death, of cardiac failure/senile decay).

29. Houghton le Spring district (Durham), 1874, 10a: 589, no. 90 (birth); Sunderland district (Durham), 1956, 1a: 943, and conversation with John Harrison's grandson in March 2011; Houghton le Spring district (Durham), 1897, 10a: 639, no. 112 (marriage).

30. Houghton le Spring district (Durham), 1875, 10: 649, no. 125 (birth).

31. Guisborough district (Yorkshire—North Riding), 1871, 9d: 483, no. 133 (birth); Durham district (Durham), 1894, 10a: 498, no. 81 (marriage).

32. Easington district (Durham), 1868, 10a: 385, no. 334 (birth).

33. *Parish register transcripts for Wakefield, 1600–1812,* Family History Library film 098,549 (birth and baptism); Leeds district (Yorkshire—West Riding), 1884, 9b: 390, no. 405 (William's death, of chronic cerebral disease—paralysis); Joseph, 64 (2nd marriage); *Bishops' transcripts for St. Peter's Church, Leeds, 1631–1837,* Family History Library film 0918,381 (Sarah's birth and parentage); Joseph, 67 (Sarah's death); Leeds district (Yorkshire—West Riding), 1838, 23: 283, no. 188 (1st marriage).

34. *Bishops' transcripts for St. Peter's Church, Leeds, 1631–1837,* Family History Library film 0918,377 (birth and baptism); Hunslet district (Yorkshire—West Riding), 1859, 9b: 163, no. 11 (death, of obstructed bowel and peritonitis).

35. *Births and baptisms of Leeds, Independent Church, 1756–1837,* Family History Library film 0828,139 (birth and baptism); Leeds district (Yorkshire—West Riding), 1874, 9b: 401, no. 56, and Joseph, 64 (death, of cardiac asthma and albuminuria); Leeds district (Yorkshire—West Riding), 1838, 23: 471, no. 68 (marriage).

36. *Bishops' transcripts for St. Peter's Church, Leeds, 1631–1837,* Family History Library film 0918,379 (baptism); Leeds district (Yorkshire—West Riding), 1888, 9b: 327, no. 296 (death, of heart disease).

37. *Births and baptisms of Leeds, Arian Independent Church, 167?–1837,* Family History Library film 0828,138 (birth and baptism); Leeds district (Yorkshire—West Riding), 1884, 9b: 381, no. 382 (death, of disease of heart); will of Francis Lupton, proved at Wakefield 20 June 1884 (death); Lupton, 44, 64–66; Newcastle upon Tyne district (Northumberland, Tyne and Wear), 1847, 25: 363, no. 29 (marriage).

38. *Parish register transcripts of Hanover Square Chapel, 1781-1844,* Family History Library film 095,016 (birth and baptism); Leeds district (Yorkshire—West Riding), 1892, 9b: 398, no. 266 (death, of diabetes exhaustion); estate of Frances Elizabeth Lupton, administration at Wakefield 20 April 1892; *Oxford Dictionary of National Biography,* 60 vols. (Oxford and New York, 2004), 34: 782–83; Lupton, 84–88.

39. *Oxford Dictionary of National Biography,* 34: 782-83; Lupton, 86.

40. *Parish registers for All Saints Church, Worcester, 1560–1950,* Family History Library film 0354,328 (birth and baptism); York district (Yorkshire), 1887, 9d: 30, no. 442 (death, of senile decay); will of the Reverend Thomas Davis, proved at Wakefield 9 Feb. 1888 (death); Joseph Foster, *Alumni Oxonienses: The members of the University of Oxford, 1715–1886: their parentage, birthplace, and year of birth, with a record of their degrees. Being the matriculation register of the University, alphabetically arranged, revised and annotated,* 4 vols. (London, 1887–88), 1: 351; Lupton, 157; *The Gentleman's Magazine* 168 [1840]: 201 (marriage).

41. *Parish registers for Holy Trinity Church, Stratford-upon-Avon, 1558–1902,* Family History Library film 1067,508 (birth and baptism); Leeds district (Yorkshire—West Riding), 1899, 9b: 364, no. 387 (death, of natural decay); will of Christiana Maria Davis, proved at Wakefield in 1899; Hobbs, 157.

42. London Metropolitan Archives, Saint Mary, Newington, Register of baptisms, P92/MRY (birth and baptism); West Ham district (Essex, Greater London), 1898, 4a: 172, no. 207 (death, of apoplexy and chronic rheumatism); Lambeth district (Surrey, Greater London), 1847, 4: 266, no. 282, and London Metropolitan Archives, Saint Mark, Kennington, Register of marriages, P85/MRK (marriage).

43. London Metropolitan Archives, Saint Mary At Lambeth, Register of baptisms, P85/MRY1 (baptism); West Ham district (Essex, Greater London), 1900, 4a: 183, no. 416 (death, of morbus cordis [heart disease]).

44. *Parish registers for Parish Church of Cheshunt, 1559–1911,* Family History Library film 0991,311 (birth and baptism); West Ham district (Essex, Greater London), 1886, 4a: 89, no. 306 (daughter's marriage; the death of John Elliott was registered in the West Ham district of Essex in Oct.–Dec. 1884); Lambeth district (Greater London, Surrey), 1843, 4: 283, no. 371 (marriage).

45. *Bishops' transcripts for St. Mary's Church, Newington, 1813–1837,* Family History Library film 0307,696 (birth and baptism); Bethnal Green district (Middlesex, Greater London), 1871, 1c: 174, no. 231 (death, of disease of liver and ascites).

46. In 1841, the household of John Robison on Nelson Street, east side of New Road in Mile End Old Town, Stepney, consisted of John Robison, messenger, 35; his wife Mary, 29; their children John, 8, James, 6, and Mary, 2; Elizabeth George, 24; and John McCarthy, 30, soup maker, and Mary McCarthy, 25 ([HO107/712/4], 25 [accessed on Ancestry.co.uk]); the death of a John Cockburn Robinson [*sic*] was registered in the City of London in April–June 1850); *Parish registers for Irvine, 1677–1854,* Family History Library film 1041,384 (marriage).

47. Mary Robison household, 1881 U.K. Census, Essex, Walthamstow [RG11/1731], 57 (accessed on Ancestry.co.uk); England Census (birth place); West Ham district (Essex, Greater London), 1895, 4a: 198, no. 208 (death, of senile decay).

48. Edward Gee household, 1871 U.K. Census, Lincolnshire, Sutton St. Mary [RG10/3167], 13 (accessed on Ancestry.co.uk); Louth district (Lincolnshire), 1883, 7a: 333, no. 37 (death, of paralysis and exhaustion); Bethnal Green district (Middlesex, Greater London), 1846, 2: 12, no. 55 (marriage).

49. *Bishops' transcripts for Holy Trinity Church, Coventry, 1662–1848* Family History Library film 0502,210 (baptism).

50. John Goldsmith household, 1881 U.K. Census, London, Islington, Islington East [RG11/253], 18 (accessed on Ancestry.co.uk); Islington district (Middlesex, Greater London), 1888, 1b: 236, no. 114 (death, of internal strangulation of [hernia?]); Shoreditch district (Middlesex, Greater London), 1850, 2: 417, no. 85 (marriage).

51. Patron submission (naming her as Hester Jones), Family History Library film 1395,681; Islington district (Middlesex, Greater London), 1885, 1b: 288, no. 92 (death, of Bronchitis 5 Days).

52. London Metropolitan Archives, Saint Nicholas, Chiswick: Hounslow, Transcript of baptisms, marriages and burials, 1819 Jan.–1819 Dec., DL/DRO/BT (birth and baptism); Fulham district (Middlesex, Greater London), 1893, 1a: 48, no. 423 (death, of hepatic disease 6 months / exhaustion 1 month); Brentford district (Middlesex), 1845, 3: 1, no. 136 (marriage).

53. London Metropolitan Archives, Saint Nicholas, Chiswick: Hounslow, Transcript of baptisms, marriages and burials, 1819 Jan.–1819 Dec., DL/DRO/

BT (baptism); Fulham district (Middlesex, Greater London), 1899, 1a: 164, no. 138 (death of cardiac disease 6 months / syncope).

54. *Bishops' transcripts for Randwick, 1607–1812,* Family History Library film 0417,151 (birth); Upton upon Severn district (Worcestershire), 1881, 6c: 179, no. 367 (death, of apoplexy sanguineous); will of Miles Tugswell Chandler, proved at Worcester 7 Dec. 1882; Gloucester district (Gloucestershire), 1844, 11: 320, no. 179 (marriage).

55. *Parish registers for Upton-upon-Severn 1546–1972,* Family History Library film 0942,934 (baptism); Upton upon Severn district (Worcestershire), 1896, 6c: 198, no. 301 (death, of cancer of the liver and pancreas).

56. *Parish registers for Brewham, 1659–1902,* Family History Library film 1526,376 (baptism); Eton district (Buckinghamshire), 1867, 3a: 269, no. 349 (death, of apnea / emphysema of lungs 3 days / bronchitis).

57. *Parish registers for Iver, 1605–1827,* Family History Library film 0919,234 (birth); Eton district (Buckinghamshire), 1886, 3a: 415, no. 318 (death, of cardiac Disease / bronchitis).

58. John Harrison household, 1881 U.K. Census, Durham, Hetton le Hole [RG11/4975], 26-27 (accessed on Ancestry.co.uk); Houghton le Spring district (Durham), 1889, 10a: 274, no. 187 (death, of phthisis pulmonis, 2 years / asthma), and Joseph, 22 (death, of tuberculosis); Durham district (Durham), 1860, 10: 363, no. 452 (marriage).

59. John Harrison household, 1881 U.K. Census, Durham, Hetton le Hole [RG11/4975], 26-27 (accessed on Ancestry.co.uk); Houghton le Spring district (Durham), 1881, 10a: 230, no. 115 (death, of phthisis pulmonalis, 6 months), and Joseph, 21–22 (death, of tuberculosis).

60. Sunderland district (Durham), 1844, 24: 307, no. 38 (birth); the death of Thomas Hill, 56 [*sic*?], was registered at Sunderland in Oct.–Dec. 1902; Sunderland district (Durham), 1869, 10a: 615 (marriage).

61. Stockton district (Durham, Yorkshire—North Riding), 1848, 24: 255 (birth); the death of Elizabeth Hill, 41, was registered in the Houghton le Spring district of Durham in Jan.–March 1890.

62. *The parish register of Lythe,* Family History Library film 0990,050 (birthdate and baptism); Pedigree Resource File AFN: P8R9-4K, submitted by Prof. Alan R. Wellburn of Carnforth, Lancashire (birthplace); the death of Joseph Temple, 76, was registered in the Guisborough district of Yorkshire in Jan.–March 1910; Guisborough district (Yorkshire), 1870, 9d: 724, no. 291 (marriage).

63. Kings Lynn district (Norfolk), 1851, 13: 186, no. 292 (birth); the death of Harriet Temple, 69, was registered in the Guisborough district in July–Sept. 1921.

64. Joseph Myers household, 1811 U.K. Census, Durham, Tudhoe [RG11/4958], 18 (accessed on Ancestry.co.uk); the death of Joseph Myers, 73, was registered in the Durham City district of County Durham in July–Sept. 1904; Northallerton district (Yorkshire—North Riding), 1850, 24: 559, no. 93 (marriage).

65. Pedigree Resource File AFN: 1R96-M38, submitted by Thomas Hutchinson of South Ruslip, Middlesex (birth); Joseph Myers household, 1891 U.K. Census, Durham, Tudhoe [RG12/4101], 18 (accessed on Ancestry.co.uk)

66. Leeds district (Yorkshire—West Riding), 1838, 23: 283, no. 188; International Genealogical Index patron submission of Vaughn Edward Hunsaker from parish registers, Family History Library film 0471,817 (marriage).

67. Leeds district (Yorkshire—West Riding), 1838, 23: 283, no. 188. A John Hardman Ward married Margaret Breacewell at the Church of St. Peter-at-Leeds 30 Dec. 1805 (*Bishops' transcripts for St. Peter's Church, Leeds, 1631–1837,* Family History Library film 0918,377).

68. Margaret Ward household, 1841 U.K. Census, Yorkshire, Leeds [HO107/1346/3], 11 (accessed on Ancestry.co.uk).

69. A John Asquith married Mary Simpson at the Church of St. Peter-at-Leeds 30 Nov. 1806 (*Bishops' transcripts for St. Peter's Church, Leeds, 1631–1837,* Family History Library film 0918,377).

70. Mary Asquith household, 1841 U.K. Census, Yorkshire, Leeds, West Leeds [HO107/2321], 27 (accessed on Ancestry.co.uk).

71. *Bishops' transcripts for St. Peter's Church, Leeds, 1631–1837,* Family History Library film 0918,375 (birth and baptism), 0918,377 (marriage); Lupton, 38, 40–41 (death).

72. *Births and baptisms of Leeds, Arian Independent Church, 167?–1837,* Family History Library film 0828,138 (birth and baptism); Lupton, 45 (death and burial); will of Anne Lupton, proved at Wakefield 9 Sept. 1865 (death).

73. Lupton, 38.

74. *Parish registers of Christ Church (Tynemouth, Northumberland), 1607–1941,* Family History Library film 1068,907 (birth and baptism); Leeds district (Yorkshire—West Riding), 1881, 9b: 340, no. 332 (death, of simple decay of nature); will of Thomas Michael Greenhow, proved at Wakefield 17 Nov. 1881 (burial); Lupton, 33, 72–74; Leeds district (Yorkshire—West Riding), 1854, 9b: 478, and *The Publications of the Thoresby Society,* vol. 5, George Denison Lumb, ed., *The Registers of the Parish Church of Adel, in the county of York from 1606 to 1812,* 111 (2nd marriage); *Births and baptisms of Leeds, Arian Independent Church, 167?–1837,* Family History Library film 0828,138 (Anne's birth and baptism); Leeds district (Yorkshire—West Riding), 1905, 9b: 332 (Anne's death); "Monumental/Memorial Inscriptions St. John's Church, Roundhay, South Section" (http://homepage.ntlworld.com/nev.hurworth/South.html) (Thomas and Anne's burial inscriptions*); Bishops' transcripts for the Archdeaconry of Norwich, 1685–1925* Family History Library film 1278,921 (1st marriage).

75. *Births and baptisms of Norwich, Octagon Presbyterian Church, 1691–1837,* Family History Library film 0825,333 (birth and baptism); Newcastle-upon-Tyne district (Northumberland, Tyne and Wear), 1850, 25: 238, no. 319 (death, of phthisis pulmonaris); *The Publications of the Harleian Society, Visitation Series,* vol. 39, John W. Clay, ed., *Familiae Minorum Gentium: Diligentiâ Josephi Hunter, Sheffieldiensis, S.A.S.,* 1108; Peter Townend, *Burke's Genealogical and Heraldic History of the Landed Gentry,* 3 vols. (London, 1965), 3: 621.

76. Lupton, 72–80.

77. *Parish registers for St. Helen's Church, Worcester, 1538–1939,* Family History Library film 0354,311 (baptism); Tewkesbury district (Worcestershire), 1845, 11: 395, no. 81, and *The Gentleman's Magazine* 177 [1845]: 325–26 (death, of a violent cold); *Alumni Oxonienses,* 1: 350; Hobbs, 155, 156; *The Gentleman's Magazine* 86 [1799]:77 (marriage).

78. *Parish registers for St. Clement Danes, 1558–1948,* Family History Library film 0574,266 (birth and baptism); Hobbs, 8, 15 (birth, marriage, death), 156 (death).

79. Hobbs, 15 (birth and death); *The Parish Register Society,* vol. 16, Richard Savage, trans., *The Registers of Stratford-on-Avon in the County of Warwick, Marriages 1558–1812,* 215 (marriage).

80. DR 724/6/2/10/(4), Shakespeare Centre Library and Archive, The National Archives (birth); DR 266/14, Shakespeare Centre Library and Archive, The National Archives (baptism); Hobbs, 15 (death).

81. Thomas Glassborow household, 1851 U.K. Census, Middlesex, St. Bartholomew Exchange [HO107/1532], 27 (accessed on Ancestry.co.uk); Guildhall, St. Andrew Holborn, Register of baptisms, 1792–1805, P69/AND2/A/01/Ms6667/14 (1795 baptism); Shoreditch district (Middlesex), 1860, 1c: 158, no. 44 (death, of phthisis); London Metropolitan Archives, Saint Mary At Lambeth, Register of marriages, P85/MRY1 (marriage).

82. Thomas Glassborow household, 1851 U.K. Census, Middlesex, St. Bartholomew Exchange [HO107/1532], 27 (accessed on Ancestry.co.uk); Shoreditch district (Middlesex), 1864, 1c: 193, no. 158 (death, of natural decay/ jaundice).

83. Lambeth district (Surrey, Greater London), 1847, 4: 175, no. 367 (death, of cholera); London Metropolitan Archives, Saint Mary At Lambeth, Register of marriages, P85/MRY1 (marriage).

84. *Parish registers for St. Martin-in-the-Fields, Westminster, 1550–1926,* Family History Library film 0561,144 (birth and baptism); Lambeth district (Surrey, Greater London), 1848, 4: 215, no. 499 (death, of phthisis 1 year).

85. Lambeth district (Greater London, Surrey), 1843, 4: 283, no. 371.

86. Lambeth district (Greater London, Surrey), 1843, 4: 283, no. 371.

87. International Genealogical Index patron submission, Family History Library film 0456,549 (baptism); *Old parochial registers for Douglas, 1691–1855,* Family History Library film 0102,903 (marriage).

88. Elizabeth Gee household, 1851 U.K. Census, Lincolnshire, Sutton St. Mary [HO107/2097], 56 (accessed on Ancestry.co.uk); *London, England, Marriages and Banns, 1754-1921* (database on Ancestry.com) (marriage); will of William Gee, Victualler of Dorset Place, Westminster, Middlesex, dated 16 Dec. 1846, proved 15 April 1852 (death).

89. Will of William Gee, Victualler of Dorset Place, Westminster, Middlesex, dated 16 Dec. 1846, proved 15 April 1852 (death).

90. Bethnal Green district (Middlesex, Greater London), 1846, 2: 12, no. 55.

91. *Bishops' transcripts for St. Mary's Church, Newington, 1813–1837,* Family History Library film 0307,696 (daughter's baptism).

92. Joseph, 37 (death, of stomach cancer).

93. Rebecca Goldsmith household, 1851 U.K. Census, Middlesex, Islington, Islington East [HP107/1617], 31 (accessed on Ancestry.co.uk); Maidstone district (Kent), 1870, 2a: 413, no. 97 (death, of bronchitis); Joseph, chart following 269 (maiden name).

94. Shoreditch district (Middlesex, Greater London), 1850, 2: 417, no. 85.

95. *Parish registers for St. Thomas' Church, Winchester, 1678–1876,* Family History Library film 1041,222 (baptism); Brentford district (Middlesex), 1845, 3: 1, no. 136 (son's marriage); *London, England, Marriages and Banns, 1754–1921* (database on Ancestry.com) (marriage).

96. Brentford district (Middlesex), 1845, 3: 1, no. 136 (daughter's marriage); *London, England, Marriages and Banns, 1754–1921* (database on Ancestry.com) (marriage).

97. London Metropolitan Archives, Saint Nicholas, Chiswick: Hounslow, Transcript of Baptisms and Burials, 1839 Jan.–1839 Dec., Dl/DRO/BT (burial).

98. *Parish registers for Stonehouse, 1558–1867,* Family History Library film 0856,954 (marriage); Gloucester district (Gloucestershire), 1844, 11: 320, no. 179 (son's marriage).

99. Miles Chandler household, 1851 U.K. Census, Worcestershire, Leigh [HO107/2041], 34 (accessed on Ancestry.co.uk).

100. Gloucester district (Gloucestershire), 1844, 11: 320, no. 179.

101. *Parish registers for Upton-upon-Severn, 1546–1972* Family History Library film 0942,934 (daughter's baptism).

102. *Parish registers for Brewham, 1659–1902,* Family History Library film 1526,376.

103. *Parish registers for Iver, 1605–1827,* Family History Library film 0919,234 (daughter's baptism).

104. James Harrison household, 1851 U.K. Census, Durham, Moorsley [HO107/2393], 23 (accessed on Ancestry.co.uk) (same for marriage); Durham district (Durham), 1866, 10a: 203, no. 203 (death, of morbus hepatis [liver disease] some time, ascites 14 days).

105. James Harrison household, 1851 U.K. Census, Durham, Moorsley [HO107/2393], 23 (accessed on Ancestry.co.uk); Joseph, 19 (death, of consumption [tuberculosis]).

106. Anthony Liddle household, 1851 U.K. Census, Durham, Sherburn [HO107/2391], 20 (accessed on Ancestry.co.uk); Durham district (Durham), 1838, 24: 68, no. 38 (marriage).

107. Anthony Liddle household, 1851 U.K. Census, Durham, Sherburn [HO107/2391], 20 (accessed on Ancestry.co.uk); Durham district (Durham), 1896, 10a: 229, no. 358 (death, of senile decay).

108. William Hill household, 1851 U.K. Census, Durham, Sunderland, East Sunderland [HO107/2397], 7 (accessed on Ancestry.co.uk); Sunderland district (Durham, Tyne and Wear), 1875, 10a: 445, no. 235 (death, of pneumonia 4 days); Sunderland district (Durham, Tyne and Wear), 1838, 24: 212, no. 390 (marriage).

109. Sunderland district (Durham, Tyne and Wear), 1880, 10a: 327, no. 111 (death, of apoplexy).

110. Elizabeth Webster household, 1871 U.K. Census, Durham, Bishop Wearmouth, North Bishop [RG10/5002], 62 (accessed on Ancestry.co.uk); Sunderland district (Durham, Tyne and Wear), 1840, 24: 206, no. 352 (marriage).

111. Elizabeth Webster household, 1881 U.K. Census, Durham, Ryton [RG11/5046], 37 (accessed on Ancestry.co.uk).

112. Guisborough district (Yorkshire—North Riding), 1880, 9d: 358, no. 148 (death, of senile decay).

113. Pedigree Resource File AFN: P8RG-QC, submitted by Prof. Alan R. Wellburn of Carnforth, Lancashire (birth); Guisborough district (Yorkshire—North Riding), 1880, 9d: 321, no. 54 (death, of senile decay, anasarca).

114. *Parish registers for St. Mary's Church, Sprowston, 1673–1915,* Family History Library film 1526,886 (baptism); the death of Samuel Stone, 49, was registered in the Guisborough district of Yorkshire in Oct.–Dec. 1867; Guisborough district (Yorkshire), 1870, 9d: 724, no. 291 (daughter's marriage); Henstead district (Norfolk), 1845, 13: 329, no. 73 (marriage).

115. *Parish registers of Hethersett, 1615–1915,* Family History Library film 0152,886 (baptism); Guisborough district (Yorkshire—North Riding), 1909, 9d: 308, no. 392 (death, of senile decay).

116. Northallerton district (Yorkshire—North Riding), 1850, 24: 559, no. 93.

117. The death of Robert Swales, 74, was registered in the Northallerton district of Yorkshire in July–Sept. 1875.

118. Pedigree Resource File AFN: 1R96-M22, submitted by Thomas Hutchinson of South Ruslip, Middlesex (birth).. The death of a Sarah Swales, 85, was registered in the Bradford district of Yorkshire in Oct.–Dec. 1884.

119. *The Luptonian* 33 [1984]: 16 (birth and baptism); International Genealogical Index patron submission, Family History Library film 0457,837 (death and marriage places); *The Registers of the Parish Church of Adel, in the county of York from 1606 to 1812*, 5: 111; Lupton, 15, 21–27, 32–33.

120. *Births and baptisms of Leeds, Arian Independent Church, 167?–1837,* Family History Library film 0828,138 (birth and baptism); International Genealogical Index patron submission (death); Lupton, 25.

121. As transcribed by Dr. C. A. Lupton, Lupton, 22.

122. Lupton, 38. A John Darnton, son of John, was baptized at Call Lane Arian Congregation, Leeds, Yorkshire 29 Dec. 1752 (*Births and baptisms of Leeds, Arian Independent Church, 167?–1837,* Family History Library film 0828,138). A John Darnton married Anne Healey at the Church of St. Peter-at-Leeds 28 July 1777 (*Bishops' transcripts for St. Peter's Church, Leeds, 1631–1837,* Family History Library film 0918,375).

123. *Births and baptisms of Leeds, Arian Independent Church, 167?–1837,* Family History Library film 0828,138 (daughter's baptismal record).

124. Lupton, 38.

125. Lupton, 71 (birth and death); *Parish registers of Christ Church, Tynemouth, Northumberland, 1607–1941,* Family History Library film 1068,928 (marriage).

126. *Parish registers of Christ Church, Tynemouth, Northumberland, 1607–1941,* Family History Library film 1068,653 (baptism); Lupton, pedigree facing 71.

127. Lupton, 71.

128. *Births and baptisms of Norwich, Octagon Presbyterian Church, 1691–1837,* Family History Library film 0825,333 (baptism); International Genealogical Index patron submission, Family History Library film 0177,957; *Familiae Minorum Gentium,* 39: 1108 (gives date of death as June 1827); *Burke's Genealogical and Heraldic History of the Landed Gentry,* 1965, 3: 620.

129. *Parish register transcripts of St. John's Church, 1587–1812,* Family History Library film 095,015 (baptism); Kings Norton district (Staffordshire, Warwickshire, Worcestershire), 1848, 18: 269, no. 84 (death, of old age and decay with irregular action of the heart but without ascertainable disease), and *The Gentleman's Magazine* 184 [1848]: 445.

130. Lupton, pedigree facing 67.

131. *Oxford Dictionary of National Biography*, 37: 19–24; http://www25.uua.org/ uuhs/duub/articles/jamesmartineau.html, accessed 31 Jan. 2011.

132. *Oxford Dictionary of National Biography*, 37: 13–19; http://en.wikipedia.org/ wiki/Harriet_Martineau, accessed 31 Jan. 2011.

133. Lupton, 155 (birth and death); *Parish registers for Newland, 1741–1899,* Family History Library film 0856,960 (marriage).

134. Hobbs, 155 (death).

135. Hobbs, 154, and H. Pirie-Gordon, *Burke's Genealogical and Heraldic History of the Landed Gentry* (London, 1937), 2113 (death). *The Gentleman's Magazine* 86 [1799]: 910, notes the death of William Stable, jun., 23, in Worcester, the son of "Mr. S.[,] glover, in the Strand [in London]" 20 Oct. 1799.

136. Worcester district (Hereford and Worcestershire), 1847, 18: 490, no. 155 (death, of age of debility).

137. Hobbs, 4 (birth), 7 (death), 8 (marriage).

138. Hobbs, 7, 8.

139. Hobbs, 15; DR 724/6/2/10/(4), Shakespeare Centre Library and Archive, The National Archives (marriage).

140. Hobbs, 15, 16.

141. Guildhall, St. Andrew Holborn, Register of Baptisms, 1792–1805, P69/ AND2/A/01/Ms6667/14 (baptism of Thomas Glassborrow).

142. *Parish registers of St. Giles Cripplegate Church, London, 1559–1936,* Family History Library film 0380,207 (birth); Bishopsgate district (London, Middlesex), 1837, 2: 66, no. 11 (death); *Parish registers for St. Anne's Church, Soho, 1686–1931,* Family History Library film 0918,596 (marriage).

143. International Genealogical Index patron submission, Family History Library film 0452,872 (baptism), 0456,549 (son's baptism).

144. *Parish registers for St. Thomas' Church, Winchester, 1678–1876,* Family History Library film 1041,222 (son's baptism).

145. *London, England, Marriages and Banns, 1754–1921* (database on Ancestry.com).

146. *London, England, Marriages and Banns, 1754–1921* (database on Ancestry.com).

147. Durham district (Durham), 1838, 24: 68, no. 38.

148. Sunderland district (Durham, Tyne and Wear), 1838, 24: 212, no. 390.

149. *Parish register transcripts, St. Michael's Church, Bishop–Wearmouth, 1567–1924,* Family History Library film 091,083 (marriage).

150. *Parish register transcripts of Sunderland, 1719–1879,* Family History Library film 091,115 (baptism); the death of Isabella Dixon, 80, was registered in the Sunderland district of Durham in April–June 1874.

151. Sunderland district (Durham, Tyne and Wear), 1840, 24: 206, no. 352.

152. Sunderland district (Durham, Tyne and Wear), 1865, 10a: 253, no. 62 (death, of apoplexia, worn out, old age, as Jane Bowie).

153. *The parish register of Lythe,* Family History Library film 0990,050 (marriage).

154. *Parish registers for Southacre, 1292–1904,* Family History Library film 2262,678 (birth and baptism); *Parish registers for St. Mary's Church, Sprowston, 1673–1915,* Family History Library film 1526,137 (marriage).

155. Samuel Stone household, 1841 U.K. Census, Norfolk, Sprowston [HO107/783/17], 2 (accessed on Ancestry.co.uk).

156. The death of a Joseph Middleton was registered in the Henstead district of Norfolk in April–June 1844; *Parish registers of Hethersett, 1615-1916,* Family History Library film 1526,887 (marriage).

157. Pedigree Resource File AFN: 1R95-FPS, submitted by Thomas Hutchinson of South Ruslip, Middlesex; *Bishops' transcripts for Hawnby, 1608-1852,* Family History Library film 0990,786 (marriage).

158. Pedigree Resource File AFN: 1R95-FQ1, submitted by Thomas Hutchinson of South Ruslip, Middlesex; *Parish registers for Bilsdale, 1590-1812,* Family History Library film 0573,985 (baptism).

159. *The Publications of the Thoresby Society,* vol. 13, George Denison Lumb, ed., *Leeds Parish Registers, 1695–1713,* 27 (birth and baptism); *The Luptonian* 50 [1988]: 14 and Lupton, 11 (death).

160. *The Registers of the parish church of Leeds,* Family History Library film 0599,919 (birth and baptism); *The Luptonian* 50 [1988]: 14 and Lupton, 11 (death).

161. Lupton, 25, pedigree; *Parish register transcripts, 1701–1837, Parish Church of Whitkirk,* Family History Library film 098,543 (marriage).

162. *Births and baptisms of Leeds, Arian Independent Church, 167?–1837,* Family History Library film 0828,138 (baptism and death, from her daughter's date of birth).

163. *Bishops' transcripts for Hutton-Magna, 1680–1860,* Family History Library film 0207,543 (baptism); Lupton, pedigree facing 71, and *Transcripts of parish registers of London, St. Bartholomew the Less, London, 1547–1837,* Family History Library film 0416,744 (1st marriage); Lupton, 71 (2nd marriage), and *Parish registers of Allhallows the Less, London, England,* Family History Library film 0374,338 (baptism of daughter Jane).

164. *Parish register transcripts of St. Hilda's Church, 1653–1812,* Family History Library film 091,132 (marriage).

165. William John Charles Moens, *The Walloons and their church at Norwich, 1565–1832* (Lymington, 1888), 128 (baptism and marriage), 130, 133 (death and burial); *Familiae Minorum Gentium,* 39: 1107 (baptism and death); *Burke's Genealogical and Heraldic History of the Landed Gentry,* 1965, 3: 618.

166. *Parish registers for St. George Colegate Church, Norwich, 1538–1952,* Family History Library microfilm 0993,666 (birth and baptism); *Familiae Minorum Gentium,* 39: 1107 (baptism, on 22 Feb. 1725), 1130 (death); Moens, 130, 133 (death and burial); Lupton, 67.

167. *Anna Letitia Barbauld: Selected Poetry and Prose* (Peterborough, Ont., 2001), 149–50.

168. *Church records, 1726–1923, John Knox Presbyterian Church,* Family History Library film 087,983 (birth and baptism); *The Publications of the Durham and Northumberland Parish Register Society,* vol. 1, Herbert Maxwell Wood, ed., *The Registers of Whickham, in the County of Durham: Marriages, 1579–1812,* 97 (marriage).

169. *Parish register transcripts, 1587–1812, St. John's Church,* Family History Library film 095,014 (baptism); *Parish registers of All Saints Church, Newcastle-upon-Tyne, 1600–1940* Family History Library 1068,966 (death).

170. *Burke's Genealogical and Heraldic History of the Landed Gentry,* 1937, 2113; Hobbs, 152.

171. *The registers of St. Benet and St. Peter, Paul's Wharf, London, 1607–1837,* Family History Library film 0845,242 (marriage).

172. Hobbs, Table B, 4. See note 200, p. 136, on the unlikely number of generations between Jonathan Hobbs (b. 1736) and his grandfather Charles (1596–1700).

173. Hobbs, 4. This seems anachronistic, since Mary (Matthews) Hobbs' son was born in 1736, almost eighty years after Cromwell's death – her brother would have had to be born during the first quarter of the seventeenth century.

174. Hobbs, Table C, 6.

175. Hobbs, Table F1, 13.

176. *Parish registers for St. Clement Danes, 1558–1948,* Family History Library film 0574,460 (marriage).

177. *Old Parochial Registers of Lesmahagow, Lanarkshire* 649/00 0030 0071 (marriage).

178. *Parish register transcripts of Sunderland and various other parishes in Durham and Northumberland, 1719–1879,* Family History Library film 091,115 (baptisms of Isabella Stafford, 1794, and Jonas Stafford, Jr., 1804).

179. *Parish registers for Southacre, 1292–1904,* Family History Library film 2262,678 (son Samuel's baptism).

180. Pedigree Resource File AFN: 1R94 5FM (death); *Parish registers for Kirby-in-Cleveland, 1627–1949,* Family History library film 0894,248 (marriage).

181. Pedigree Resource File AFN: 1R94-5SW (birth and death).

182. *Parish register transcripts, 1552–1715, Chapelry of Pateley-Bridge,* Family History Library film 098,551 (baptism); *The Luptonian* 33 [1984]: 16 and Lupton, 2, 9 (death); *The Registers of the Parish Church of Adel, in the county of York from 1606 to 1812,* 5: 111 (marriage).

183. *The Registers of the Parish Church of Adel, in the county of York from 1606 to 1812,* 5: 49 (baptism); *The Luptonian* 50 [1988]: 13 and Lupton, 2, pedigree (death).

184. Lupton, 11. "George, base begotten son of Rebecca Dawson, of Low^r Headrow, by Arthur Hickson," was baptized at the Church of St. Peter-at-Leeds 27 Nov. 1710 (*Leeds Parish Registers, 1695–1713,* 13: 79).

185. Lupton, pedigree (death); *Leeds Parish Registers, 1695–1713,* 13: 119 (marriage).

186. *The Publications of the Thoresby Society,* vol. 10, George Denison Lumb, ed., *The Registers of the Parish Church of Leeds from 1667 to 1695,* 252 (baptism); Lupton, pedigree (death).

187. *The Registers of the Parish Church of Leeds from 1667 to 1695,* 10: 257 (baptism); Lupton, pedigree.

188. *Births, baptisms, deaths and burials of Leeds, Presbyterian Church, 1650–1837, Mill Hill Chapel,* Family History Library 0828,139 (baptism); Lupton, pedigree (death).

189. *Bishops' transcripts for Kirkby-Ravensworth, 1663–1869,* Family History Library film 0207,550 (baptism); *Bishops' transcripts for Hutton-Magna, 1680–1860,* Family History Library film 1849,307 (burial); Lupton, 71 (marriage).

190. *The registers of the parish church of Grinton in Swaledale, Co.York,* Family History Library film 0897,351 (baptism).

191. *Parish registers for Lowestoft, 1561–1717,* Family History Library film 097,130 (marriage).

192. Moens, 128 (birth and baptism), 130, 133 (death and burial); *Familiae Minorum Gentium,* 39: 1107, 1130; *Burke's Genealogical and Heraldic History of the Landed Gentry,* 1965, 3: 617; *Parish registers, 1538–1945, St. George-Tombland Church,* Family History Library film 1596,459 (marriage).

193. *Parish registers, 1538–1945, St. George-Tombland Church,* Family History Library film 1596,459 (baptism); *Parish registers of Bramerton, 1561–1902,* Family

History Library film 1565,305 (2nd marriage); *Familiae Minorum Gentium*, 39: 1107, 1130; Moens, 130; Lupton, pedigree.

194. *Familiae Minorum Gentium*, 39: 1130; *Parish registers for St. George Colegate Church, Norwich, 1538–1952*, Family History Library film 0993,666 (baptism of daughter Margaret).

195. *Parish registers for St. George Colegate Church, Norwich, 1538–1952*, Family History Library film 0993,666 (baptism); *Familiae Minorum Gentium*, 39: 1130, 1134.

196. *Parish Registers for Gateshead, 1559–1960*, Family History Library film 0252,779 (marriage). Robert Rankin [No. 302] and Ann Cole [No. 303] named one of their sons William Burdon Rankin (*Parish register transcripts of Hanover Square Chapel, 1781–1844*, Family History Library film 095,016).

197. *Burke's Genealogical and Heraldic History of the Landed Gentry*, 1937, 2113; Hobbs, 150.

198. *Parish registers for Elstree, 1585–1945*, Family History Library film 1040,873 (marriage).

199. *Parish registers for Elstree, 1585–1945*, Family History Library film 1040,873 (baptism).

200. Hobbs, 3 (he died after falling down a flight of stairs). As a source, Hobbs is problematic for the first two generations, as Charles (1596–1700) could hardly be the grandfather, and Thomas Hobbs (b. ca. 1625–55) the father, of someone born in 1736.

201. Hobbs, Table C, 6.

202. *Parish registers for St. Giles' Church, Reading, 1518–1894*, Family History Library microfilm 088,342 (baptism); *Parish registers for Swallowfield, 1636–1853*, Family History Library film 0291,666 (marriage); John Wintrip, "William Davenport of Reading," research report February 2011.

203. *Parish registers for Maple-Durham, 1627–1867*, Family History Library film 0887,483 (baptism); Hobbs, Table F1 (2nd marriage).

204. *Old parochial registers for Lesmahagow, 1692–1854*, Family History Library film 1066,597 (baptism of younger children).

205. *Old Parochial Registers for Lesmahagow, Lanarkshire* 649/00 0030 0031 (marriage).

206. Pedigree Resource File AFN: 1R94-5N3 (death); *Parish registers for Kirby-in-Cleveland, 1627–1949*, Family History Library film 0894,248 (marriage).

207. *Parish registers for Kirby-in-Cleveland, 1627–1949* Family History Library film 0894,248 (baptism); Pedigree Resource File AFN: 1R95-CZ4 (death).

208. *The Registers of the Parish Church of Adel, in the county of York from 1606 to 1812*, 5, 6 (baptism), 127 (burial); Lupton, 3.

209. *The Registers of the Parish Church of Leeds from 1612 to 1639*, 3: 158 (baptism), 207 (burial); Lupton, 3.

210. Lupton, pedigree.

211. *The Registers of the Parish Church of Leeds from 1667 to 1695*, 10: 252

212. *The Registers of the Parish Church of Leeds from 1667 to 1695*, 10: 257 (son's baptism); Lupton, pedigree.

213. *Births, baptisms, deaths and burials of Leeds, Presbyterian Church, 1650–1837, Mill Hill Chapel*, Family History Library 0828,139 (baptism of daughter Olove).

214. Lupton, pedigree.

215. *Parish registers for Forcett, 1596–1901*, Family History Library film 0468,805 (marriage at Forcett); *The registers of the parish church of Grinton in Swaledale, Co. York* Family History Library film 0897,351 (daughter's baptism at Grinton).

216. *Familiae Minorum Gentium*, 39: 1107; *Burke's Genealogical and Heraldic History of the Landed Gentry*, 1965, 3: 617.

217. Moens, 133.

218. *Oxford Dictionary of National Biography*, 19: 571 (birth and death); *Parish registers for St. John the Baptist Church, Lakenham, 1568–1901*, Family History Library film 1526,493 (marriage).

219. "Notes on the Family of Mackerell of Norwich, No. II," *The East Anglian; or Notes and Queries on subjects connected with the counties of Suffolk, Cambridge, Essex, and Norfolk*, New Series, 13: 141.

220. Edgar Taylor, *The Suffolk Bartholomeans: A memoir of the ministerial and domestic history of John Meadows, Clk., A.M., formerly fellow of Christ's College, Cambridge . . .* (London, 1840), 3 (birth), 3, 19, 24 (1st marriage), 22 (1st wife's death), 73 (2nd marriage), 86 (3rd marriage), 87 (3rd wife's death); *Oxford Dictionary of National Biography*, 37: 656; *Familiae Minorum Gentium*, 39: 1127, 1130 (birth and baptism).

221. The *Suffolk Bartholomeans*, 81 (death), 88 (burial).

222. *Familiae Minorum Gentium*, 39: 1134.

223. *Parish registers for Elstree, 1585–1945*, Family History Library film 1040,873 (baptism of son Robert).

224. *The registers of marriages of St. Mary le Bone, Middlesex, and Oxford Chapel*, Family History Library film 0845,261 (marriage); John Wintrip, "William Davenport of Reading," research report February 2011.

225. "William Davenport of Reading," research report February 2011.

226. *Parish registers for Maple-Durham, 1627–1867*, Family History Library 0887,483 (burial).

227. *Parish registers for Maple-Durham, 1627–1867,* Family History Library film 0887,483 (burial).

228. *Old Parochial Registers for Lesmahagow, Lanarkshire* 649/00 0030 0031.

229. Pedigree Resource File AFN: 1R95-CQN.

230. Lupton, 3.

231. Lupton, 3, pedigree.

232. Lupton, 3.

233. *Burke's Genealogical and Heraldic History of the Landed Gentry*, 1965, 3: 617.

234. *Proceedings of the Huguenot Society of London*, 4: 354; *Bulletin de la Commission pour l'histoire des églises Wallonnes,* 4: 354.

235. *Oxford Dictionary of National Biography*, 19: 570–71; *The parish registers of Warrington*, Family History Library film 0844,815 (marriage).

236. "The Family of Mackerell of Norwich, No. II," New Series, 13: 141–42.

237. "The Family of Mackerell of Norwich, No. II," New Series, 13: 142; *Parish registers of St. Peter Mancroft parish, Norwich, 1538–1997,* Family History Library film 1565,790 (death).

238. *The Suffolk Bartholomeans*, 4a, 17; *Familiae Minorum Gentium*, 39: 1129.

239. *The Suffolk Bartholomeans*, 74.

240. *The Suffolk Bartholomeans,* 64a (birth, death, 1st marriage), 72 (2nd marriage); Joseph Foster, comp., *Pedigrees of the County Families of Yorkshire*, 3 vols. (London, 1874), 1: Pedigree of Fairfax of Gilling Castle, Denton.

241. *Familiae Minorum Gentium*, 39: 1134.

242. William Betham, *The Baronetage of England, or, the History of the English Baronets, and Such Baronets of Scotland, as Are of English Families: With Genealogical Tables, and Engravings of Their Armorial Bearings; Collected from the Present Baronetages, Approved Historians, Public Records, Authentic Manuscripts, Well Attested Pedigrees, and Personal Information*, 5 vols. (Ipswich, 1801–5), 4: 142.

243. Pedigree Resource File from Karen D. Thomson of Newlands, Wellington, New Zealand.

244. Lupton, 3.

245. *Burke's Genealogical and Heraldic History of the Landed Gentry*, 1965, 3: 617.

246. *Proceedings of the Huguenot Society of London*, 4: 356.

247. *Oxford Dictionary of National Biography*, 19: 570.

248. "Notes on the Family of Mackerell of Norwich," *The East Anglian*, New Series, 13: 108–9.

249. "Notes on the Family of Mackerell of Norwich," New Series, 13: 109; "Notes on the Family of Mackerell of Norwich, No. II," New Series, 13: 142.

250. *Parish Register of St. George Tombland, Norwich* 1538–1707, Family History Library film 094,947 (baptism); "Notes on the Family of Mackerell of Norwich, No. II," New Series, 13: 141–42; Francis Blomefield, *An essay towards a topographical history of the county of Norfolk: containing a description of the towns, villages, and hamlets, with the foundations of monasteries, churches, chapels, chantries, and other religious buildings. . . ,* 11 vols. (London, 1805–10), 4:196.

251. *Familiae Minorum Gentium*, 39: 1127.

252. L. G. Pine, *The New Extinct Peerage, 1884–1971* (London, 1972), 189.

253. *The Suffolk Bartholomeans* 4, 4a (says 1675); *Pedigrees of the County Families of Yorkshire*, 1: Pedigree of Fairfax of Gilling Castle, Denton (says 1676).

254. *The Suffolk Bartholomeans*, 64a.

255. *Familiae Minorum Gentium*, 39: 1134.

256. Lupton, 3

257. "The Family of Mackerell of Norwich," New Series, 13: 109; "The Norwich Dutch Church. Early Records of Baptisms, 1598–1619," *The East Anglian*, New Series, 13: 179.

258. *Parish Register of St. George Tombland, Norwich 1538–1707*, Family History Library film 094,947.

259. *The Suffolk Bartholomeans*, 64a; Joseph Foster, *Pedigrees of the County Families of Yorkshire*, 1: Pedigree of Fairfax of Gilling Castle, Denton; *Parish registers for St. Michael Coslany Church, Norwich, 1558-1963*, Family History Library film 099,658 (marriage). John Fairfax is confused with his nephew in *Suffolk Bartholomeans*, where he is called a son of William and Lucy (Goodman) Fairfax, who married at Great Shelford, Cambridgeshire 29 Nov. 1560 (*Parish register transcripts, 1557–1844, Parish Church of Great Shelford*, Family History Library film 0990,398). This couple is treated in *The Visitation of Norfolk, 1563, 1589, and 1613*, 118, and John Fairfax is called their fifth son: it would seem unlikely that such a son could have married in 1580, nineteen years after his parents' marriage. John Fairfax is correctly identified in Foster's pedigree, although Foster was not certain which of the senior William Fairfax's marriages – to Anne Baker and Katherine Tanfield – produced him.

260. *Pedigrees of the County Families of Yorkshire*, 1: Pedigree of Fairfax of Gilling Castle, Denton.

261. *Oxford Dictionary of National Biography*, 18: 928; *An essay towards a topographical history of the county of Norfolk*, 5: 121.

262. Lupton, 3.

263. *The Suffolk Bartholomeans* 64a, 65 (see note 259, p. 139, about a mistaken generation); *Pedigrees of the County Families of Yorkshire*, 1: Pedigree of Fairfax of Gilling Castle, Denton (which gives a marriage date of 26 Oct. 1542 to Anne Baker); *Index to the marriage registers of St. Mary's, Bury St. Edmunds, 1537–1837*, Family History Library film 0993,231, which says 26 Oct. 1541 (first marriage); Douglas Richardson and Kimball G. Everingham, *Plantagenet Ancestry: A Study in Colonial and Medieval Families* (Baltimore, 2004), 302.

264. *The Suffolk Bartholomeans*, 64a; Charles Webster, ed., *Health, medicine, and mortality in the sixteenth century* (Cambridge, 1979), 221–22; *Pedigrees of the County Families of Yorkshire*, 1: Pedigree of Fairfax of Gilling Castle, Denton, incorrectly calls Mary's father John Birch.

265. *Plantagenet Ancestry*, 302; *Yorkshire Archeological Journal* 19 [1907]: 185–87, Inquisition Post Mortem of Sir Thomas Fairfax of Walton, Knt., 1521, taken at Newburgh, Jan. 20, 12 Hen. VIII (1520–21): Thomas Fayrefax died Dec. 1, 12 Hen. VIII (1520). Nicholas, his son and next heir, then aged 21¾ and upwards (Escheator's Inquisitions, City of York, 11–12 Hen. VIII, File 272).

BIBLIOGRAPHY

Books
(see also Serials)

Elizabeth Saunders Arbuckle, ed., *Harriet Martineau's Letters to Fanny Wedgwood* (Stanford, 1983)

Anna Letitia Barbauld: Selected Poetry and Prose (Peterborough, Ont., 2001)

William Betham, *The Baronetage of England, or, the History of the English Baronets, and Such Baronets of Scotland, as Are of English Families: With Genealogical Tables, and Engravings of Their Armorial Bearings; Collected from the Present Baronetages, Approved Historians, Public Records, Authentic Manuscripts, Well Attested Pedigrees, and Personal Information*, 5 vols. (Ipswich, 1801–5)

Francis Blomefield, *An essay towards a topographical history of the county of Norfolk: containing a description of the towns, villages, and hamlets, with the foundations of monasteries, churches, chapels, chantries, and other religious buildings...*, 11 vols. (London, 1805–10)

Frederic Boase, *Modern English Biography...*, 6 vols. (Truro, 1892–1921; reprinted in 1965)

Joseph Foster, *Alumni Oxonienses: The members of the University of Oxford, 1715–1886: their parentage, birthplace, and year of birth, with a record of their degrees. Being the matriculation register of the University, alphabetically arranged, revised and annotated*, 4 vols. (Oxford and London, 1887–88)

Joseph Foster, comp., *Pedigrees of the County Families of Yorkshire*, 3 vols. (London, 1874)

Claudia Joseph, *Kate: Kate Middleton, Princess in Waiting* (New York, 2009)

C. A. Lupton, *The Lupton Family in Leeds* (Leeds, 1965)

F. M. Lupton, *Descendants of Charles Hobbs, 1596–1700* (Leeds, 1914)

William John Charles Moens, *The Walloons and their church at Norwich, 1565–1832* (Lymington, 1888)

Oxford Dictionary of National Biography, 60 vols. (Oxford and New York, 2004)

L. G. Pine, *The New Extinct Peerage, 1884–1971* (London, 1972)

H. Pirie-Gordon, *Burke's Genealogical and Heraldic History of the Landed Gentry* (London, 1937)

Douglas Richardson and Kimball G. Everingham, *Plantagenet Ancestry: A Study in Colonial and Medieval Families* (Baltimore, 2004)

Leslie Stephen and Sidney Lee, *Dictionary of National Biography*, 66 vols. (London, 1885–1901)

Edgar Taylor, *The Suffolk Bartholomeans: A memoir of the ministerial and domestic history of John Meadows, Clk., A.M., formerly fellow of Christ's College, Cambridge...* (London, 1840)

Peter Townend, ed., *Burke's Genealogical and Heraldic History of the Landed Gentry*, 18th ed., 3 vols. (London, 1965)

Charles Webster, ed., *Health, medicine, and mortality in the sixteenth century* (Cambridge, 1979)

Serials
(see also Books)

Bulletin de la Commission de l'histoire des églises Wallonnes, 8 vols. (1885–1892)

The East Anglian; or Notes and Queries on subjects connected with the counties of Suffolk, Cambridge, Essex, and Norfolk, 17 vols. in 2 series (1858–1900)

New series, volume 13, "Notes on the Family of Mackerell of Norwich"

New series, volume 13, "Notes on the Family of Mackerell of Norwich, No. II"

New series, volume 13, "The Norwich Dutch Church. Early Records of Baptisms, 1598–1619"

The Parish Register Society, 76 vols. (1896–1917)

Volume 16, Richard Savage, trans., *The Registers of Stratford-on-Avon, Co. Warwick*

Proceedings of the Huguenot Society of London, 47 vols. (1887–1961)

The Publications of the Durham and Northumberland Parish Register Society, 36 vols. (1898–1926)

Volume 1, Herbert Maxwell Wood, ed., *The Registers of Whickham, in the County of Durham: Marriages, 1579–1812*

Publications of The Harleian Society, Visitation Series, 117 vols. (1869–1977)

Volume 32, Walter Rye, ed., *The Visitation of Norfolk, 1563, 1589, and 1613*

Volume 39, John W. Clay, ed., *Familiae Minorum Gentium: Diligentiâ Josephi Hunter, Sheffieldiensis, S.A.S.*

The Publications of the Thoresby Society, 59 vols. (1891–1986)

Volume 1, *Leeds Parish Church Registers, 1571–1612*

Volume 3, George Denison Lumb, ed., *The Registers of the Parish Church of Leeds from 1612 to 1639*

Volume 5, George Denison Lumb, ed., *The Registers of the Parish Church of Adel, in the county of York from 1606 to 1812*

Volume 7, George Denison Lumb, ed., *The Registers of the Parish Church of Leeds from 1639 to 1667*

Volume 10, George Denison Lumb, ed., *The Registers of the Parish Church of Leeds from 1667 to 1695*

Volume 13, *Leeds Parish Registers, 1695–1713*

Journals

The Clifton Magazine, 2007

The Gentleman's Magazine, 302 vols. (1731–1868)

The Luptonian, 53 numbers (1974–1989)

Yorkshire Archeological Genealogical Journal, 82 vols. to date (1869–)

Volume 19, John Filson, F.S.A., "Gilling Castle"

Newspapers

The Daily Mail, 23 March 2009 and 17 Nov. 2010 [online edition]

The Guardian, 23 Nov. 2010 [online edition]

The Sun, 5 Aug. 2006

The Sunday Express, 12 Dec. 2010 [online edition]

The Telegraph, 17 Nov. 2010 [online edition]

The Times, 19 July 1887

Research Report

John Wintrip, "William Davenport of Reading," February 2011

Microforms

Parish registers for Bilsdale, 1590–1812, Family History Library film 0573,985

Parish register transcripts, St. Michael's Church, Bishop-Wearmouth, 1567–1924, Family History Library film 091,083

Parish registers of Bramerton, 1561–1902, Family History Library film 1565,305

Parish registers for Brewham, 1659–1902, Family History Library film 1526,376

Parish registers for Parish Church of Cheshunt, 1559–1911, Family History Library film 0991,311

Bishops' transcripts for Holy Trinity Church, Coventry, 1662–1848, Family History Library film 0502,210

Old parochial registers for Douglas, 1691–1855, Family History Library film 0102,903

Parish registers for Elstree, 1585–1945, Family History Library film 1040,873

Parish registers for Forcett, 1596–1901, Family History Library film 0468,805

Parish Registers for Gateshead, 1559–1960, Family History Library film 0252,779

Parish register transcripts, 1557–1844, Parish Church of Great Shelford, Family History Library film 0990,398

The registers of the parish church of Grinton in Swaledale, Co. York, Family History Library film 0897,351

Parish register transcripts of Hanover Square Chapel, 1781–1844, Family History Library film 095,016

Bishops' transcripts for Hawnby, 1608–1852, Family History Library film 0990,786

Parish registers of Hethersett, 1615–1916, Family History Library film 1526,887

Bishops' transcripts for Hutton-Magna, 1680–1860, Family History Library films 0207,543 and 1849,307

Parish registers for Irvine, 1677–1854, Family History Library film 1041,384

Parish registers for Iver, 1605–1827, Family History Library film 0919,234

Parish registers for Kirby-in-Cleveland, 1627–1949, Family History Library film 0894,248

Bishops' transcripts for Kirkby-Ravensworth, 1663–1869, Family History Library film 0207,550

Church records, 1726–1923, John Knox Presbyterian Church, Family History Library film 087,983

Parish registers for St. John the Baptist Church, Lakenham, 1568–1901, Family History Library film 1526,493

The Registers of the parish church of Leeds, Family History Library film 0599,919

Births and baptisms of Leeds, Arian Independent Church, 167? –1837, Family History Library film 0828,138

Births and baptisms of Leeds, Independent Church, 1756–1837, Family History Library film 0828,139

Births, baptisms, deaths and burials of Leeds, Presbyterian Church, 1650–1837, Mill Hill Chapel, Family History Library film 0828,139

Bishops' transcripts for St. Peter's Church, Leeds, 1631–1837, Family History Library films 0918,375, 0918,377, and 0918,381

Old parochial registers for Lesmahagow, 1692–1854, Family History Library film 1066,597

Parish registers of Allhallows the Less, London, England, Family History Library film 0374,338

Transcripts of parish registers of London, St. Bartholomew the Less, London, 1547–1837, Family History Library film 0416,744

The registers of St. Benet and St. Peter, Paul's Wharf, London, 1607–1837, Family History Library film 0845,242

Parish registers of St. Giles Cripplegate Church, London, 1559–1936, Family History Library film 0380,207

Parish registers for Lowestoft, 1561–1717, Family History Library film 097,130

The parish register of Lythe, Family History Library film 0990,050

Parish registers for Maple-Durham, 1627–1867, Family History Library film 0887,483

Parish registers of All Saints Church, Newcastle-upon-Tyne, 1600–1940, Family History Library 1068,966

Bishops' transcripts for St. Mary's Church, Newington, 1813–1837, Family History Library film 0307,696

Parish registers for Newland, 1741–1899, Family History Library film 0856,960

Bishops' transcripts for the Archdeaconry of Norwich, 1685–1925, Family History Library film 1278,921

Births and baptisms of Norwich, Octagon Presbyterian Church, 1691–1837, Family History Library film 0825,333

Parish registers for St. George Colegate Church, Norwich, 1538–1952, Family History Library film 0993,666

Parish Register of St. George Tombland, Norwich 1538–1707, Family History Library film 094,947

Parish registers for St. Michael Coslany Church, Norwich, 1558–1963, Family History Library film 0993,658

Parish registers of St. Peter Mancroft parish, Norwich, 1538–1997, Family History Library film 1565,790

Parish register transcripts, 1552–1715, Chapelry of Pateley-Bridge, Family History Library film 098,551

Bishops' transcripts for Randwick, 1607–1812, Family History Library film 0417,151

Parish registers for St. Giles' Church, Reading, 1518–1894, Family History Library film 088,342

Parish registers for St. Clement Danes, 1558–1948, Family History Library films 0574,266 and 0574,460

Parish registers, 1538–1945, St. George-Tombland Church, Family History Library film 1596,459

Parish register transcripts of St. Hilda's Church, 1653–1812, Family History Library film 091,132

Parish register transcripts, 1587–1812, St. John's Church, Family History library films 095,014 and 095,015

The registers of marriages of St. Mary le Bone, Middlesex, and Oxford Chapel, Family History Library film 0845,261

Parish registers for St. Anne's Church, Soho, 1686–1931, Family History Library film 0918,596

Parish registers for Southacre, 1292–1904, Family History Library film 2262,678

Parish registers for St. Mary's Church, Sprowston, 1673–1915, Family History Library films 1526,137 and 1526,886

Parish registers for Stonehouse, 1558–1867, Family History Library film 0856,954

Parish registers for Holy Trinity Church, Statford-upon-Avon, 1558–1902, Family History Library film 1067,508

Parish register transcripts of Sunderland, 1719–1879, Family History Library film 091,115

Parish registers for Swallowfield, 1636–1853, Family History Library film 0291,666

Parish registers of Christ Church, Tynemouth, Northumberland, 1607–1941, Family History Library films 1068,653, 1068,907, and 1068,928

Parish registers for Upton-upon-Severn, 1546–1972, Family History Library film 0942,934

Parish register transcripts for Wakefield, 1600–1812, Family History Library film 098,549

The parish registers of Warrington, Family History Library film 0844,815

Parish registers for St. Martin-in-the-Fields, Westminster, 1550–1926, Family History Library film 0561,144

Parish register transcripts, 1701–1837, Parish Church of Whitkirk, Family History Library film 098,543

Parish registers for St. Thomas' Church, Winchester, 1678–1876, Family History Library film 1041,222

Parish registers for All Saints Church, Worcester, 1560–1950, Family History Library film 0354,328

Parish registers for St. Helen's Church, Worcester, 1538–1939, Family History Library film 0354,311

Guildhall Archives

St. Andrew Holborn, Register of Baptisms, 1792–1805 (P69/AND2/A/01/Ms6667/14)

London Metropolitan Archives

Saint Nicholas, Chiswick: Hounslow, Transcript of baptisms, marriages and burials, 1819 Jan.–1819 Dec. (DL/DRO/BT)

Saint Nicholas, Chiswick: Hounslow, Transcript of Baptisms and Burials, 1839 Jan.–1839 Dec. (Dl/DRO/BT)

Saint James The Great, Hackney, Register of baptisms (P79/JSG)

Saint Peter, Hackney, Register of Baptisms (P79/PET)

Saint Mark, Kennington, Register of marriages (P85/MRK)

Saint Mary At Lambeth, Register of baptisms (P85/MRY1)

Saint Mary, Newington, Register of baptisms (P92/MRY)

Online databases

England & Wales, National Probate Calendar [Index of Wills and Administrations], 1861–1941 (database on Ancestry.com)

Leeds Grammar School Admission Books: 1820 to 1900 (database at Google Books)

London, England, Marriages and Banns, 1754–1921 (database on Ancestry.com)

UK, Soldiers Died in the Great War (database on Ancestry.co.uk)

Wills and Estate Administrations

Will of Miles Tugswell Chandler, proved at Worcester 7 Dec. 1882

Will of Christiana Maria Davis, proved at Wakefield in 1899

Will of the Reverend Thomas Davis, proved at Wakefield 9 Feb. 1888

Will of William Gee, Victualler of Dorset Place, Westminster, Middlesex, dated 16 Dec. 1846, proved at Canterbury 15 April 1852

Will of Constance Glassborow, proved at Oxford 21 Oct. 1977

Will of Frederick George Glassborow, proved at London 16 Sept. 1954

Will of Frederick John Glassborow, proved at London 13 Jan. 1933

Will of Thomas Michael Greenhow, proved at Wakefield 17 Nov. 1881

Will of Anne Lupton, proved at Wakefield 9 Sept. 1865

Estate of Frances Elizabeth Lupton, administration at Wakefield 20 April 1892

Will of Francis Lupton, proved at Wakefield 20 June 1884

Will of Francis Martineau Lupton, proved at Wakefield 10 July 1921

Will of Olive Christiana Middleton, proved at London 3 Feb. 1937

Will of Richard Noël Middleton, proved at London 23 Oct. 1951

Will of Gavin Fullarton Robison, proved at London 24 April 1925

INDEX